مى يامب
ابسملتى

PROfILES OF

Successful

Asian

Women

compiled by Yasmin Sheikh

Yasmin Sheikh
15 Ederline Avenue
Norbury
London sw16 4rz

First published 1996
© Yasmin Sheikh, 1996

Design and typesetting by
Lionel Openshaw

Published with the help of a Heritage
Publications Grant from Croydon
Council. For more information on the
HPG contact Jess Steele, Heritage
Publications & Research Officer,
Croydon Clocktower, Katharine Street,
Croydon CR9 1ET.

ISBN 1 898536 51 1

British Library Cataloguing in
Publication Data.
A catalogue record for this book is
available from the British Library.

Printed and bound in Great Britain by
Biddles Ltd, Guildford and King's Lynn

Forewords

Rt Hon The Baroness
Shreela Flather JP DL

I am grateful to Yasmin for giving me the opportunity to say a few words about these profiles of Asian women. As an Asian woman myself I am proud to be included along with so many others who have made a contribution to the life of their adopted country. It is easy for Asian women to be overlooked when thinking about the impact that ethnic minorities have had on this country. For that reason alone anything that brings to the forefront the sheer variety of the women's achievement is something to be applauded. I hope this book will be widely used to raise our profile.

Councillor Mary Walker,
London Borough of Croydon

I am delighted to welcome this informative publication which Yasmin Sheikh has assembled painstakingly over a period of time. It is of great importance that young Asian women have role models when they attend school, college and university and this directory, setting out the contribution made by Asian women in the United Kingdom, will be an added spur to their endeavours. I am sure it will find a place on bookshelves in public libraries and in colleges and universities throughout the country. I am particularly pleased to see many Croydon Asian women represented here.

Dame Angela Rumbold MP

It gives me very great pleasure to write a foreword to this directory. Yasmin Sheikh has worked hard to draw together the contributions of a number of Asian women living and working in this country. These women have made a significant contribution to the economy and welfare of this country and deserve universal recognition. It is also important that there should be public acknowledgement of the achievements of the Asian community as demonstrated by their women to the life and promotion of the United Kingdom.

Contents

Subject Index

Acknowledgments

I wish to thank and acknowledge my friends and relatives, whose support and co-operation has made this dream come true.

Elvira Gregory's support gave me a tremendous start and I am most grateful to her.

My thanks to the Sheikh family, namely, Riaz, Parveen, Ijaz, Tariq, Roohi, Rizwan, Nabeel, Romana, Douglas, Tamur, Humera and Farah, who gave me encouragement at every stage which, I can assure you, I needed as I had many difficulties to overcome.

It is my great pleasure to mention Susan Hallam and Dr Khowaja Mousa – without their help this publication would not exist.

Last but not least, I am proud of and indebted to the Borough of Croydon Council for their sympathetic and professional approach in this venture.

Special thanks to Mary Walker for giving the right guidance and advice.

Not So Silent! Profiles of Successful Asian Women is dedicated to my children ROMANA SHEIKH and NABEEL SHEIKH who have been so supportive and a tower of strength to me.

Yasmin Sheikh, October 1996

Introduction

In 1992 Dr K Mousa and I were deep in conversation discussing Asians who had achieved success in the UK. To our surprise, we found that a great many of our successful friends were Asian women.

I then mentioned to my friend Dame Angela Rumbold DBE MP, an idea I had been mulling over which was to compile a directory of Asian women focusing on their successful contributions to the community. She encouraged me to make my idea a reality, for this I am grateful.

It was to be called *The Silent Contributors* but when Baroness Shreela Flather remarked, "we're not so silent!" I had to agree and the new title was born.

The project from conception to final product has taken four years. However, it has been an uplifting and enlightening experience for me, providing an opportunity to meet Asian women from all walks of life. Many have made their mark through hard work and by struggling against all odds. Some of the women achieved success at a young age.

It is a timely reminder to society that Asian women come not only from India or Pakistan but from a wide variety of countries which include Sri Lanka, Malaysia, Africa and the Middle East as well as UK-born. What binds these women together are the hurdles they have had to overcome to achieve success. As a result they have become even stronger.

I hope that the profiles collected here will be of interest to a range of audiences such as pupils in schools, students in colleges and universities, professionals and non-professionals, employers as well as employees.

Finally, I know that the benefit to Asian women will be unparalleled because they themselves will receive motivation from a group with similar background and experiences. This does not, however, diminish the benefits to everybody; men and women, Asian and non-Asian.

Information has been extracted from the profiles which were sent to me and every care has been taken to ensure that important details were not omitted. Due to late entries or restrictions of space, I was unable to include all the profiles in this edition. I hope to include them in our next edition.

At the end of this book there is a form that can be photocopied, completed and sent to me for future publications. I would like to express my apologies in advance for any omissions or mistakes.

The personal choice of some women not to include their photographs has been respected.

Shama Ahmad

Fluent in *Hindi, Urdu, Punjabi, English*

Religion *Muslim*

My Journey

I was born in Pakistan. My parents migrated from India to Pakistan after Partition. I was married in 1970 to Mr Mahmood Ahmad. I now have two daughters and three sons. My daughters' names are Ambrain and Nosheen. My sons' names are Kashif, Wasif and Sharaf. I also have two sons-in-law whose names are Sohail Qureshi and Zahir Ahmad.

Social work was always a hobby in primary and secondary schools. I was always involved in school functions and unions. I passed matriculation and gained Secondary School Certificate in 1965 from CB School, Wah Cantt.

In 1967 I passed the Intermediate Certificate in Government Women's College in Rawalpindi.

In 1970 I studied at West Ham Community College for Arts and Crafts and English Literature.

From 1971 to 1972 I attended a college for Arts and Crafts.

For my BA training I served for three months as a teacher in Rose Girls High School and KG Burney School as a temporary Headteacher in Rawalpindi.

My Life in Britain

For a number of years I have been involved in a local business and social welfare work.

After the murder of Akthar Ali Beg, myself and my husband felt there was a need for a Muslim Centre in the London Borough of Newham. Subsequently, we had a letter published in *Voice of the Time*. As a result of that publication, we gathered people together and involved ourselves deeply in social work.

In 1984 I became a member of the Labour Party and on 3rd May 1990 was elected as a member of Newham Council. Prior to my election to the Council I taught Urdu in Monega School to the new Muslim Citizens Association.

Achievements & Contributions

In 1989 I was elected as a school governor for Cleves Road School, E6. At present I am also a governor for Plashet School and the Vice-chairperson of the governing body.

I am a member of the Leisure Services Committee and hold the position of Vice-chairperson of Race on that committee.

I served as Deputy Mayor for the Municipal Year 1993/94.

Lalita Ahmed

Fluent in	*Hindu, Urdu, Bengali, English*

Religion	*Hindu*

My Journey

I was born in Lucknow, India. I am graduate from Lucknow University with a Science degree.

I was the first television presenter on *Doordarshan* Indian Television. I am a gold medallist in dancing and winner of two scholarships from the Government of Uttar Pradesh for English and Science.

My Life in Britain

I came to Britain in 1961. I presented television programmes on the BBC and World Service radio in 1961 – 1992. I have written six books on cookery. I am married with three children.

Achievements & Contributions

Presenter of programmes on BBC TV and Radio.

Chairperson of UK Asian Women's Conference 1980 – 1983.

Trustee of Academy of Indian Dance.

Writer of cookery books.

Five films – 55 *Columns, The Big Battalion, A Kind of English, Wild West and Bhaji on the Beach*.

First presenter of Spectrum Radio now Radio Asia.

Personal Interests

Social work relating to Asian community and old people. Music, reading, travel and, of course, cooking.

Najma Akhtar

Fluent in	*Urdu, English*

Religion	*Muslim*

My Journey

I was born and brought up in Chelmsford, UK. My parents were from Uttar Pradesh. They moved to London about 22 years ago. This was a real culture shock because Chelmsford was small and quiet whereas London is large, busy and noisy. Although I've now been to India and Pakistan, I still feel England to be my home.

My Life in Britain

My primary education was in Chelmsford and the rest of my education was completed in London.

I studied as a Chemical Engineer at the South Bank University and went on to do an MSc at Aston University in Birmingham. My musical career actually unconsciously started whilst I was still doing my degree in Engineering when I won the Asian Song Contest in 1984.

Achievements & Contributions

After I won the Asian Song Contest, I went to India in 1986 where the Film Music Director Ravi recorded an album of Ghazal music for me. By that time I had recorded a number of songs for the BBC and two Indian magazine programmes. I was now winning acclaim.

I recorded with a UK-based record label in 1987 to produce a Ghazal/Indo/Jazz arrangement. There was a big explosion in world music awareness and I hit the music headlines. In 1988 I was the first Asian to perform at Ronnie Scott's Jazz Venue.

I have recorded with Andy Summer from the band Police, Steve Coleman (Jazz saxophonist from New York) and Jah Wobble UK.

In 1989 my second album was released and I started touring the world.

I have set a trend within the Asian music scene and serve as a role model for young Asians growing up in the West.

In 1991 I recorded the music for a Japanese TV commercial and also released on my own record label an album titled *Pukar*.

In 1992 I appeared in Channel Four's *Family Pride* and four times at the London Jazz Café plus numerous TV appearances such as *01 for London*.

Personal Interests

Jogging, tennis, swimming, and listening to music from all over the world, but especially Indian classical music. I like to help people and am involved with certain charities.

My Journey

I was born in Badaun, Uttar Pradesh, India. I achieved my primary education in Badaun. I remember my early youth with my mother going out helping people in social need. I began writing poems and short stories from very early life. My family migrated to Pakistan in 1951 and remained until I obtained British nationality. I was educated in Pakistan, obtained a BA at Karachi and practiced as a teacher in Pakistan. During my university days I took part in sports and inter-collegiate debates. I was also elected as General Secretary of Karachi Girls Students' Federation. My mother was one of the co-founders of All Pakistani Women's Association and because of this opportunity I developed political awareness and in-depth understanding of our culture.

Zohra Naseem Akhtar BEM

Fluent in *Hindi, Urdu, Sindhi, Gujarati, English*

Religion *Muslim*

My Life in Britain

1964 Obtained Postgraduate Diploma in Social Science

1965 Certificate in Marriage Guidance and Counselling

1966 Voluntary teacher in English as a second language

1968 Cookery teacher for foreign students

1969 Working as an interpreter and translator

1993 Working as an interpreter and translator

Achievements & Contributions

1969	Worked as an Urdu/Hindi programme broadcaster with BBC World Service
1971 – 1974	Founded and developed Women's Asian Cultural Organisation of Hammersmith & Fulham
1974 – 1979	I am a writer and poet and because of this personal interest I founded Asian Writers and Poets Organisation of Hammersmith & Fulham and encouraged young writers and poets in publishing their works
1980 – 1984	Co-founded and developed Asian Elderly Milap Club of Hammersmith & Fulham
1984 – 1986	Served as Chairperson of Hammersmith & Fulham Council for Racial Equality
1984 – 1989	Sat on various local educational and legal committees contributing towards multicultural and equal opportunity issues
1985 – 1987	Governor of local schools
1985 – 1988	Lay Visitor on local Lay Visitor Panel
1990	Awarded British Empire Medal, Queen's New Year Honours List, for services to the Asian community
1991	Elected to the forum which advises the council on all ethnic minority issues and matters.
	Involved with the Victim Support Group for Young and Married Women and helped to establish a 'Safe House'.
1991 – 1993	Developed a Marriage Counselling Forum for Asian women.
	I was involved in helping and advising school leavers on their career development and training.

Personal Interests

I enjoy living in Fulham. I am the only daughter in a family of seven. I have two brothers who are both barristers, a brother who is a solicitor, one who is a doctor, one who is a computer scientist and one who is in business. I have three sons and a daughter. One son is a barrister, the second is in business and the third is a journalist. My daughter works as a drama artist. I believe in the value of family life. I enjoy cooking and have published my own cookery book. My two volumes of poetry books have already been published in Pakistan.

Zaineb Alam

My Journey

I spent my youth in Karachi, Pakistan, even though I was born in Bombay in December 1952 (we moved to Karachi within a year). My childhood was comfortable and happy; I was an only daughter with five huge brothers, and received plenty of love and attention from everyone.

My formal education didn't amount to much. I regret this now, but I know I do my best to make up for it. From 15 onwards I was in love with a man who most often ignored me. I persevered and married him four years later. With this marriage my life changed dramatically as I realised that adult life was quite a daunting prospect. My childhood came to a definite end at this point in time. Within two years of marriage I had a baby girl. In 1975 I began to travel and lived in Iran and the Middle East with a short stay in Cyprus. I busied myself with normal housewife duties, but also formed small women's clubs for group activities and trips, whenever possible.

My Life in Britain

In 1976 I moved to London with my husband and child. Slowly but surely I made friends and again formed a club to keep myself busy called the 'home enjoyment club'. I had a son in 1979, but even while busy with two children I felt I needed to fill a gap. In 1980 I started a small business, selling tracksuits from my home. It proved extremely successful and taught me about customer relations, customer psychology, marketing and so on. By 1985 I had cultivated quite a curiosity for the world of fashion and business.

I opened a boutique in St John's Wood called Zee Zee's. At first it was planned to specialise in designer clothes catering to a shortage of good quality Asian clothes in London. However I realised that it would be far more practical, exciting and imaginative if these clothes could be worn in both eastern and western gatherings. Thus I set out to create an original East-West fusion.

I manufactured here and imported from abroad, indulging my imagination with French silk, Venetian lace, and hand-painted materials from all over the world. Quality was the most important thing in my styles. In 1987 I realised that I had become a pioneer in the concept of East-West fashion. I held a fashion show at the London Hilton in Park Lane; which brought me a lot of publicity and status. In 1988 I expanded and opened a second branch in High Street Kensington. Success continued and I held another major fashion show in 1989.

Achievements & Contributions

In 1988 I won the Entrepreneur of the Year Award for the Asian City Club. In 1989 I was invited to speak at the conference for the Ethnic Minority Business Initiative (EMBI) which was hosted by John Patten. During these years I did radio interviews for Radio 1 and 2, LBC and Spectrum Radio. I appeared on Network East television twice; once for an interview, and also to judge a fashion design competition. I was also interviewed on *This Morning* and provided clothes for the Channel Four series *Family Pride*. *The Independent* and *The Observer* have written large complimentary articles about Zee Zee's, and it was covered in both the 1988 and 1989 editions of the *Time Out* guide to shopping in London. Sadly in 1991 due to unavoidable circumstances, the recession and greedy landlords, Zee Zee's had to close down. At present I work in a boutique in Mayfair, as the manager of the fashion department.

I was the very first one to have started the Asian-Shalwar Kameez business, I never dreamt at the time it would take off the way it has. My career has been mentioned at length in the course book for all student fashion designers, *Chic Thrills* edited by Juliet Ash and Elizabeth Wilson and published by Pandora. My section was written by Naseem Khan. Because of this lots of young designer hopefuls come to meet me and I try to help whenever possible, trying to make them realise that fashion is a business like any other and until they see it as such life would be very difficult. When Azmat Sheikh, the winner of the Fashion Designer Award for 1993, said that she based her collection on Zee Zee and came to me for guidance "my cup runneth over"!

As for the future, I have never taken life too seriously so I can take its strange turns with ease. I know what I am capable of and am sure I will continue to busy myself in business, fashion and many other fields.

Yasmin Alibhai-Brown

Fluent in	*Kutchi, Gujarati, Swahili, English, some Hindi*
Religion	*Ismaili Muslim*

My Journey

I arrived here in 1972 at the age of 22 from Uganda, where I was born. I was part of the exodus of Asians who (most of us) were destined never to return to that lovely country. I went to school and university there and I will always recall it as a wonderful place where the local people were kind and forgiving and where everything was lush and green. However, I always felt uncomfortable about the positions we, the Asians, occupied.

My Life in Britain

Coming to Britain was partly a dream come true but also a nightmare as this was the time racism exploded outwards in a way not really seen before.

In the last 20 years I have worked as a lecturer with disadvantaged groups, a journalist writing for *The Guardian* and *The Independent, New Statesman & Society, Everywoman* and other publications, a broadcaster, and an author of several books including one on mixed relationships.

Achievements & Contributions

I am one of the very few Asian women working for national newspapers.

I also travel around the world to lecture and speak about racism and multiculturalism.

I am writing an autobiographical book which will be published later this year.

Personal Interests

I love being with my lovely daughter Leila, my extremely opinionated but loving teenage son Ari, and my husband Colin. Unfortunately, life being busy, we have too little time to spend together.

Kaushika Amin

Fluent in *Gujarati, English*

Religion *Hindu*

My Journey

I was born in Kenya, to parents who were from the Gujarat in India. I had a happy and settled childhood living with a large extended family, spanning four generations. My family and I moved to Britain in 1972 where I began my secondary education at an all-girls school in Leicester.

My Life in Britain

After leaving school I trained as a nurse at the Leicester Royal Infirmary. After four years in nursing I changed career by taking 'A' levels and gained a place at Sussex University studying Philosophy at the School of Asian and African Studies.

After university I returned to Leicester where I began work as a welfare rights adviser with a community centre in the Highfields district serving the needs of a large Asian and Afro-Caribbean population.

In 1983 I moved to London to work at the Newham Monitoring Project as a caseworker supporting people who were experiencing racial harassment. While at Newham Monitoring Project I took an MSc degree at the London School of Economics in Social Policy. My subsequent jobs included working in the *Outwrite* Women's Collective helping to produce a monthly newspaper.

In 1987 I started work as a research worker at the Runnymede Trust, a race relations research and information body. I co-authored with Robin Richardson two Runnymede Trust publications, *Politics for All: Equality, Culture and the General Election 1992* (1992) and *Multi-Ethnic Britain: Facts and Trends* (1994). In 1992 I co-authored with Carey Oppenheim *Poverty in Black and White: Deprivation and Ethnic Minorities* published by the Runnymede Trust and CPAG. I regularly contribute to journals and books. I am a co-editor of the *Runnymede Bulletin* which is published monthly and contains news and features on current issues in race relations.

Personal Interests

In 1989 I became a mother of twin daughters. Both now attend a local school. I enjoy spending time with my family, especially my children. I am also involved with many local groups including ParentLink and the Black/Jewish Forum.

Shaukat Amin

Fluent in *Hindi, Urdu, Punjabi, English*

Religion *Muslim*

My Journey

I was born in Amritsar, India. My ancestors migrated to Amritsar from Kashmir. At the time of Partition in 1947 my family moved to Lahore, Pakistan. I was fortunate enough to go to university and graduated from Stratford College for Women, Amritsar (Lahore University) in 1943, obtaining a BA in double Mathematics, English and Urdu as an optional subject. I obtained my postgraduate degree – Bachelor of Teaching – from Lahore University at the age of 20. I then worked as an Honourary Headmistress for one year as my family believed in public service. Subsequently I worked in various capacities in education and finally as Principal of Sharafabad secondary school in Karachi before coming to the UK in 1964 under the special voucher scheme. My plan was to go back after five years but as all my children were well settled in their respective schools, I was reluctant to interrupt their education.

My Life in Britain

From 1965 until 1984 I worked as a teacher in a secondary school teaching Mathematics and English.

I took early retirement in 1984 to pursue my personal interests in community service. This has become my main occupation.

1978 – 1987   Executive Committee member of National Council for Mother Tongue Teaching.

1977 to date	Chairperson of UK Asian Women's Conference, High Wycombe branch.
1984 to date	Member of Home and Water Safety Forum on Wycombe District Council. Member of Management Committee of Citizens' Advice Bureau.
1986 – 1991	External examiner RSA Diploma in Community Languages.
1988 to date	Governor of Hamilton County Middle School; Governor of Tinkerswood County Middle School; Member of Multicultural Advisory Liaison Group Bucks County Council Education Committee; and Chairperson of Asian Women's Centre.

I have also been a member of the Community Relations Forum and Ethnic Minorities Working Group on Mental Health. I am a member of High Wycombe Race Equality Education Sub-committee. I have been a trustee of the Race Equality Council since 1984, and Honourary Vice President since 1985. I am also a member of the Welfare Sub-committee. I have been a member of the management committee of the Multiracial Centre since 1989 and a member of the Spring Gardens Youth Community Centre since 1991. I am also a member of the British Federation of University Women.

Achievements & Contributions

Setting up the Asian Unit at Brenchwood School, the introduction of Urdu into the school curriculum, and the preparation of all teaching material from the alphabet to 'O' level standard prior to retirement. Founding the High Wycombe Branch of UK Asian Women's Conference, the Asian Women's Centre and Asian Elderly Day Care Centre. Holding exhibitions of Asian arts and crafts and languages. Raising the profile of ethnic minority women and elderly. Encouraging participation of Asian women in all aspects of local community activities including fundraising.

Increasing multicultural awareness within the community, promoting active liaison and understanding between the different cultural and religious groups. Raising five children who are all professionals.

I am currently a member of the Women's National Commission (WNC) and, as a representative of UK Asian Women's Conference, I attended the WNC 25th anniversary reception at 12 Downing Street in July 1994. I was awarded an MBE in the Queen's Birthday Honours List in 1994. I was delighted to receive my medal on 20th July at Buckingham Palace from Her Majesty Queen Elizabeth II.

Personal Interests

Occasionally I enjoy a game of badminton and tennis.

Jinder Aujla

My Journey

I originate from the Punjab in India but my family subsequently moved to Mombasa, Kenya. I came to England at the age of 16 leaving my family behind intending to gain a British education and pursue a worthwhile career. However things did not work out as planned as my mum died soon after I came to the UK and I had to give up the idea of studying and instead work.

My Life in Britain

In 1969 I had an arranged marriage to Jaswant with whom I had two sons, Gurdev and Harjit, who were educated in a local suburban private school. My ambition for a career started to fade as I found myself bringing up a family. However, being determined to achieve my goals, I continued my part-time computer operator job until I read an article in a national newspaper about the ever-growing financial services market under Mrs Thatcher's government. I contacted the journalist who had written the article and, to cut a long story short, soon found myself working for the Abbey Life as an associate. Now I am a member of the 'Million Dollar Round Table', the prestigious club of the élite of the insurance industry.

My main motivation is the fact that, as an Indian in a foreign country, I was always forced to recognise the fact that I could not depend on anyone to help me. I've always had to rely on my own efforts.

Achievements & Contributions

I am an active member of the Conservative Party and was nominated to run for the local elections for the Conservative Party as a councillor but did not succeed.

I have often helped in raising money for charity. In 1989 I took part in a children's charity event held in the presence of HRH Princess Margaret at the Foreign Office. I had an Indian Arts and Crafts stall which raised money for Invalid Children's Aid Nationwide. A dinner and auction event was also held during the course of the evening. The charity event raised no less than £50,000.

I am a member of the national Small Business Bureau, the Anglo-Asian Conservatives, the Finchley Business Bureau, the Indian Women's Association and the Centre for Research into Asian Migration. I am also a patron of the Finchley Friends of the Library Group.

Personal Interests

I am interested in politics and my charity work.

Talat Awais

Fluent in	*Urdu, Hindi, Punjabi, English*
Religion	*Muslim*

My Journey

I was born in Rawalpindi, Pakistan. My ancestors migrated to Pakistan from Kashmir. I spent 22 years in Pakistan. I was educated in a Government Secondary and High School. I won a scholarship due to achieving the highest marks and obtained degrees in Bachelor of Arts and Bachelor of Education from the University of Punjab. I was a teacher from kindergarten to secondary stage. I took an interest in all sorts of extra-curricular activities with complete freedom.

My Life in Britain

I worked as a technician for the Plessey Company which manufactured electronic equipment.

I joined London Transport Underground Railways as a Guard. I was offered a job in the Royal Jordan Air Line but I declined due to my marital status.

Achievements & Contributions

I was promoted to Train Driver (Train Operator) from a Guard. I was the first ever Pakistani lady driver.

I have also contributed to the programme *Asian Morning* on TV Asia.

Personal Interests

I enjoy mixing with the local community. I live in Newbury Park which is a beautiful area close to the Underground, British Rail and main shopping centres.

I enjoy cooking many types of food. I exercise to keep fit. I love to teach my children. I believe in strict discipline with kindness.

I love the latest fashions and I buy exclusive garments. I like boutiques.

I take a keen interest in and help needy people. I donate to and collect for charities for the disabled, blind, war-torn and natural disaster victims.

Nighat Banu Awan

Fluent in	*Urdu, English*

Religion	*Muslim*

My Journey

I was born in Manchester in March 1955. My ancestors are originally from Mehrut and Saharanpur in India and after the war migrated to Lahore in Pakistan. They lived there for only three years, then they migrated to Britain in 1954. I was born here and studied here. My life has been a very interesting one.

My Life in Britain

I helped with my parents' business (wholesaling and manufacturing) from a very young age. All of my family are business orientated. I have four brothers, all involved in business.

I married in March 1975. My husband is also in business. I ran a boutique for 13 years. I was involved in a lot of charity work through my shop (including fashion shows). We then went into the restaurant business in 1987.

I have three children, a son aged 18, a daughter aged 16 and a son aged seven.

Achievements & Contributions

I have suffered from crippling illnesses, such as cancer and paralysis and it made me realise that we are here for a purpose. Because of this I decided that one of my main tasks is to help the poor.

I became involved in importing. I have formed a company called Suki Int., which imports goods from Bangladesh which I retail and distribute in the UK. In this way I am helping the poor to help themselves. My achievement is to supply a whole village with employment. I have been in this business for two years; it gives me a lot of strength and satisfaction and by the grace of God it is proving successful. I have also been involved in restaurants with my husband.

Personal Interests

I love to keep fit and I am also a workaholic. It keeps my adrenaline going. Work does not seem to bother me, the more the better. Apart from that my children are my enjoyment (not forgetting my husband).

Ghazala Aziz

Fluent in   *Urdu, Hindi, English*

Religion   *Muslim*

My Journey
My parents arrived in England in 1966 from India. I was born in North London in 1967. I lived in Leytonstone until the age of 18 after which I moved with my family to Woodford Green in Essex.

My Life in Britain
My primary education was at Sebright Primary School in Hackney. My secondary education was at the Connaught Junior High School for Girls followed by Leyton Senior High School for Girls – both being comprehensive schools in Leytonstone. I studied at both Oxford and Cambridge universities. I now live and work in Oxford.

Achievements & Contributions

1983 Nine GCE 'O' levels at Grade A

1985 Four GCE 'A' levels at Grade A and two distinctions at 'S' level. After passing the Cambridge University entrance exams, I gained a place to read Medicine at Churchill College.

1986 Presented with an academic award for achieving first class honours for my first year exams by Churchill College

1988 Graduated with a BA (Hons) in Medical Sciences. Subsequently, I gained admission for my clinical studies at New College, Oxford University.

1991 Qualified from Oxford as a doctor gaining my MBB Chir qualification.

I continued to stay in Oxford at the John Radcliffe Hospital to do my houseman's year as a junior doctor. I spent three months, as part of my course, working in a hospital in India. In this year, I was also presented with an honourary MA degree from Churchill College, Cambridge.

1992 Gained a place on the GP training scheme in Oxford. I will complete my training and get my MRCGP qualification in October 1995.

Personal Interests
I have an interest in art which involves painting, visiting art galleries and collecting contemporary glassware.

I enjoy travelling and have travelled extensively. At present, I am attending Italian language classes.

I also enjoy keeping fit and go to the gym regularly. I have passed my Grade Four piano exams and like to listen to music. My other interests include cooking, dressmaking and reading.

Ramola Bachchan

Fluent in *Hindi, French, Italian, English*

Religion *Hindu*

My Journey

I was born in Calcutta, India where my parents had moved during Partition. My father was a successful Sindhi businessman and we had a 'westernised' lifestyle and upbringing. I went to boarding school at Loeto Convent, Darjeeling, when I was seven years old. I was sent to St Helen's School at Northwood in England at the age of eleven. I finished my 'O' levels and then returned to Loeto College, Calcutta where I got a degree in English Honours and Political Science. During that time, I met my husband. We dated for six years before getting married and settling down in Bombay. We had four children in quick succession.

My Life in Britain

After living in Switzerland for a year we moved to London in 1987 where we have lived ever since.

Career Development

1987 – 1989	Studied for a degree in Business Management, graduated from Webster University USA (London Campus)
1989 – 1990	CPE conversion course to become a solicitor
1990 – 1991	Law Society Solicitor Finals Course
1991 – 1992	Read for a Masters in Law at the London School of Economics
1992 – 1994	Took Articles with Lawrence Graham, a medium-sized law firm to qualify as a solicitor

Achievements & Contributions

1992 – 1994	Worked as a presenter for Radio and TV Asia
1992 to date	Have been involved with various charities in UK mainly to raise funds to help people in India
1993	Organised the Ravi Shankar Concert for Peace at the Royal Albert Hall
1993	Received several NRI awards for International Excellence
1994	Started writing as a freelance journalist for the *Asian Age*

Personal Interests

I enjoy meeting people and through the media I have made many friends in the UK. I keep fit by exercising daily. Recently I have started meditation.

I enjoy going to the theatre, listening to music, both classical and modern, Indian and western style. I enjoy travelling and doing things which contribute to the well-being of our community in the UK.

Ashwin (Usha) Bahl JP

Fluent in	*Hindi, Urdu, Gujarati, Punjabi, Swahili, English*
Religion	*Hindu*

My Journey

I was born in Nairobi, Kenya as was my mother. My father and mother's ancestors came from Sargodha which is now part of Pakistan. I spent 20 years in Kenya and worked as a teacher in Government Road Primary School for two years before migrating to England. My father was a civil servant and my maternal grandfather set up a very successful business, which is still flourishing today.

My Life in Britain

1964 – 1985	Primary school teacher with responsibility for reading in the London Borough of Enfield
Jan – Sept 86	Advisory teacher, Centre for Bilingualism, London Borough of Haringey
1986 – 1992	Primary Bilingual Co-ordinator, Multicultural Development Service, London Borough of Waltham Forest
1992 to date	Assistant Teacher-in-Charge Primary, Bilingual Support Project, London Borough of Waltham Forest

Achievements & Contributions

1984 – 1986	Member of the Task Force for Middlesex Polytechnic's, 'Reading Materials for Minority Groups' Project, which

produced dual text storybooks for primary children

1985 – 1986 Founder member of the London Borough of Enfield Inter-Faith Group

1986 Presented a paper on 'The Role of Storytelling in Schools and Libraries' at the Eleventh World Congress on Reading

1987 Presented a paper on 'Dual Text Reading Materials in Schools' at the conference organised by International Board for Books for Young People

1988 Researcher and narrator for the in-service video for teachers, *Telling Tales Together*, produced by the Cadmean Trust

1987 – 1988 Author of two children's stories *Exams Exams*, published by Nelsons, and *The Wishing Tree*, published by André Deutsch

1986 – 1989 Member of the Professional Committee of Middlesex Polytechnic Faculty of Education Performing Arts and Combined Studies

1986 – 1991 Trustee of the National Folktale and Storytelling Centre, North London

1989 to date Member of the Standing Advisory Council for Religious Education, London Borough of Waltham Forest

1990 Initiated and published a bibliography of dual text books and tapes, *Many Tales, Many Tongues*, for use in schools for primary age children

1990 to date Justice of the Peace for the North East London Area

1993 Advised, wrote for, and commissioned an educational booklet on Thalassaemia Major for UK Thalassaemia Society.

Personal Interests

I have taught Indian cookery to adults at Haringey Adult Education Centre in the Borough of Haringey for three years. I enjoy storytelling to groups of adults and children. I like swimming, walking, reading and travelling abroad.

Kamlesh Bahl

Fluent in *Hindi, English*

Religion *Hindu*

My Journey

I was born in Nairobi and moved to Britain with my Indian parents and family when I was nine years old. I was educated at Minchenden School, Southgate and went on to Birmingham University in 1977 where I gained an upper second class honours degree in law. I then studied for the Solicitors' Qualifying Examinations in London and gained distinctions in commercial law, taxation and conveyancing.

My Life in Britain

1978 – 1981	Solicitor for Greater London Council
1981 – 1984	Legal Adviser for British Steel Corporation
1984 – 1987	Solicitor at Texaco Limited
1987 – 1989	Legal and Commercial Manager at Data Logic Limited
1989 – 1993	Company Secretary and Manager Legal Services/Associate Director at Data Logic Limited
1993 to date	Legal Consultant (part-time) at Data Logic Limited

Achievements & Contributions

1988 – 1989	Chairwoman of the Law Society's Commerce and Industry Group

1989	Edited *Gazette Practice Handbook* on 'Managing Legal Practice in Business'
1989 – 1990	Member of Barnet Health Authority
1990 to date	Council Member of the Law Society
1990 to date	Non-Executive Director of Parkside Health Authority
1991 – 1992	Member of Justice Sub-Committee on Judiciary
1991 to date	Member of Ethnic Minorities Advisory Committee and Tribunals Committee (Committees of Lord Chancellor's Judicial Studies Board)
1993 to date	Member of Council of Justice
1993 to date	Member of Council and Standing Committee on Health Authorities of National Association of Health Authorities and Trusts
1993 to date	Independent Member of the Number One Diplomatic Service Appeal Board of the Foreign and Commonwealth Office

Chairwoman of Equal Opportunities Commission

Personal Interests
My leisure activities include keeping fit, swimming, Indian music and the theatre.

Lulu Bilquis Banu

Fluent in	*Bengali, Urdu, English*

Religion	*Muslim*

My Journey

I was born in Dhaka, Bangladesh on 3rd May 1927. My father was an historian and antiquarian. My mother was one of the earliest Muslim writers. I have two sisters. I married in 1953 and have two daughters.

I was in England from 1951 to 1952 for higher studies. I travelled to England again in 1967, by ship, to study at the London School of Economics and also to study Bar-at-Law. This time I travelled by ship around the Cape due to the closure of the Suez Canal. The journey took six weeks. I visited many countries in Africa on this occasion.

My Life in Britain

1951 – 1952	Studied social welfare in Manchester and also took a Postgraduate Certificate in Education from the University of London, Institute of Education
1968 – 1979	Worked as a teacher in a junior school in London
1971 – 1987	Founder member of Bangladesh Women's Association in London and continued as a member till 1987
1971 to date	Convener of the five-member Steering Committee of Bangladesh Centre, London

Achievements & Contributions

1944 – 1953	I received two Masters degrees and an LLB degree from the Dhaka University of Bangladesh. I was the first woman to receive this LLB degree. While studying for LLB I made the acquaintance of the Liberator of Bangladesh, Sheikh Mijibur Rahman, who was also studying for the degree.
1975 – 1979	Member of Asian Programme Advisory Committee of the BBC
1980 – 1984	Commissioner for the Commission for Racial Equality
1986 to date	Co-Chairperson, Bangla Academy, London.

Personal Interests

I am greatly interested in travelling. I have travelled to different countries of Europe, the Middle East, Egypt, South East Asia, Japan and America, generally to represent my country (then East Pakistan) at different international conferences.

I am interested in meeting people from different countries and of different religions. I am also interested in social work.

Shibani Basu

Fluent in *Bengali, Hindi, English*

Religion *Hindu*

My Journey

I was born in Mymensingh which is still an affluent town in Bangladesh. I grew up in a joint family headed by my grandparents. My cousin and I started going to a Government School very near to our house. After the Partition of India, we moved to Calcutta when I was only eleven. I was taken to a school in Assansal where my cousin was the headmistress. I believe that it was a perfect place for a child to grow up. Our house was just by the side of a canal and my family used to organise picnics for the children on the bank of the canal. We used to watch the boats passing by and listen to the murmur of waves and birds.

My first step into working life was as a teacher for a short period. I then left the job and joined the Ramakrishna Mission Institute of Culture Library as an Assistant Librarian. In 1966 I married and came to England for further studies.

1960   Passed the Bachelor of Arts Examination at the University of Calcutta

1962   Completed Teacher Training Course held by the Government of West Bengal

1964   Passed the Diploma in Librarianship of Calcutta

My Life in Britain
1966 – 1969   Worked in public library in London Borough of Brent

1969 – 1970	Worked in reference library in London Borough of Enfield
1975 – 1986	Worked in London Borough of Wandsworth in different libraries
1976	Passed Chartered Librarianship Examination of Library Association, UK
1986 to date	Community librarian in London Borough of Merton

Achievements & Contributions

I have wider responsibilities now as Community Librarian. I am solely responsible for promoting this service for all ethnic groups. I have the opportunity to link with various organisations in this borough. I took an active part in setting up one such organisation called Merton Asian Women Association and have been working as honourary chairperson. The association received an award from Holt Jackson Library Supplier in 1992.

From 1986	Active member of the Asian Librarian and Art Officers' Group
From 1989	Active member of the Milat Asian Housing Association
From 1990	Elected member of the Committee of Centour Housing Association

Also Vice-chairperson of CILLA (Cooperative of Indic Language Laser Authority). I attend their periodic meetings as a specialist in Bengali language and do the cataloguing and classification of all Bengali books.

From 1993	Elected as General Secretary of the Ethnic Community Centre in Vestry Hall

I also translate into Bengali important documents for the benefit of the ethnic community.

Personal Interests

I like to help people who are in need. I enjoy both music and cooking. My husband and I both keep in very close contact with our relations and friends. We also have a common interest in theatre, cinemas and travelling abroad.

Tahera Sultan Begum

Fluent in	*Urdu, Hindi, English*

Religion	*Muslim*

My Journey

I was born in Darya Ganj, Delhi in India. I was educated in the Muslim University Aligarh in India where I completed my BEd and MA in Urdu and continued to study Master of Literature at Delhi University. I started writing poetry when I was a university student. My poetry reflects feelings and emotions from different incidents in life.

I have always been interested in languages and have translated many books from English to Urdu.

My Life in Britain

I came here as a housewife. Being a teacher professionally I started teaching voluntarily at home.

Achievements & Contributions

I have written a book of Urdu poetry (*Qatra and Shabnam*) which was published in 1992. Here in London I attend Urdu poetry symposiums regularly and enjoy reading my poetry and listening to other poets.

I have been invited to read poetry in international Mushaera in India and represent UK poets in various parts of India including Delhi, Hydrabad, Calcutta and Jamshedpur.

I have also translated a few booklets into Urdu for the London Borough of Brent.

Enthusiasm for writing poetry is still there and soon my second book will be published.

Personal Interests

I enjoy sewing, knitting and cooking. I also have an interest in fabric painting. I have a wide circle of friends both in my area and far away.

Gurpreet Kaur Bhui

Fluent in *Punjabi, English*

Religion *Sikh*

My Journey

I was born in Chandigarh, India. My father came to the UK to work when I was a baby and my mother followed on when I was a year old in 1965. We settled in Croydon, Surrey which is where I went to school and gained my GCE 'O' and 'A' levels prior to going to Reading University to study Mathematics and Computer Science in 1982. At school I was very interested in music and drama and took part in many school plays. I worked as a Saturday assistant in Marks and Spencer and occasionally in the holidays as a DSS clerical assistant.

My university years were hard work but also great fun. I made very good friends and travelled abroad around Europe in the holidays with them. I left university in 1986 with a BSc Honours degree and started working in the computing industry. I have been working in this field for just over eight years. I married in 1981 and now live in Bromley, Kent.

My Life in Britain

1986 – 1989   Systems Analyst with CCL Assurance Ltd

1989 – 1994   Systems Analyst and Senior Systems Analyst with Hill Samuel Financial Services Ltd

1994 to date   Management Consultant with 121 Consulting Ltd

Achievements & Contributions

1980 Ten GCE 'O' levels, five at Grade A

1981	Grade Eight Certificate in Piano
1982	Four GCE 'A' levels, two at Grade A
1986	BSc Honours degree from University of Reading
1988	Organised a successful fund-raising fashion show
1991	Learnt Italian at evening class
1992	Certificate in Management from the Open University Business School
1994	Started working as a part-time Youth Worker with Bromley Youth Services

Personal Interests

My work currently takes up much of my time. I often have to work away from home on project work at client sites. I am responsible for configuring and installing various modules of an integrated software package called SAP. My experience within the financial services industry sector and of financial systems packages at Hill Samuel has introduced me to this particular field. My job also involves giving presentations and training courses, often to Finance Managers. Managing my own time is very important.

I swim regularly to keep fit and am a member of my local sports club. I enjoy walking in the summer. I also enjoy skiing very much and try to go whenever possible. My husband and I enjoy going to concerts, mostly popular music, and occasionally to jazz clubs. We often eat out and try different foods.

I take a full interest in the activities of my local gurdwara. In 1988, I took responsibility for organising a fund-raising fashion show for the gurdwara which raised £2,000. The programme also included ghazal singers, classical Indian dancing, comedy and food.

In addition to my full-time job, I have a keen interest in young people and have worked as a paid part-time Youth Worker. I now work voluntarily when time allows. I am also very interested in education.

Dr Qudsia Chandran
MB.BS, DRCOG (LOND)

Fluent in *Pushto, Urdu, Punjabi, English*

My Journey

I was born in Mardan, in the North West Frontier Province of Pakistan to Muslim parents. My father was a civil engineer; his prestigious job took us around NWFP and I spent my childhood living in Peshawar, Kohat, Landikotal and so on. We spent our summer holidays in Muree and Abottabad hill stations. I completed my primary education at the Presentation Convent School, Peshawar. My childhood was free and easy, and uncomplicated by political and racial problems.

I qualified as a doctor at Fatima Jinna Medical College, Lahore, the only women's medical school in Pakistan and worked in hospitals in Lahore, Peshawar and Kohat before coming to England. It was here that I met and married my husband Raj who is a Tamil from Sri Lanka. We have three children, Kannan a dental surgeon in Nottingham, Parosha, doing her bar finals at Lincoln's Inn, and Ruban studying economics, at Leeds.

My Life in Britain

1967 Worked in Doncaster Royal Infirmary and took my qualification DRCOG (Lond)

1968 My year of introduction into general practice

1969 Appointed as Principal General Practitioner in Sutton in Ashfield, Nottinghamshire in partnership with my husband

1970 Appointed as Family Planning Medical Officer.

1994 Celebrated 25 years of uninterrupted general practice in the same practice with my husband Raj. We had a grand celebration to mark this milestone and we were joined by Rt Hon Virginia Bottomley JP MP, Secretary of State for Health.

Achievements & Contributions

1973 Helped husband win District Council elections as Councillor in Ashfield

1974 Attended Queen's garden party at Buckingham Palace

1976 Involved in advising Nottingham branch of All Pakistan Women's Association on health matters of Pakistani women

1977 Elected social secretary of North Trent Division of the Overseas Doctors' Association

1987 Organised Asian Women's National Conference in London where several Ministers of State were invited to speak on national matters

1989 Helped husband Raj fight the general election as a Conservative parliamentary candidate for Preston, Lancashire

1990 Spoke on the Health Debate at the Conservative Party Conference in Brighton to over 4,000 delegates

1992 Invited to join the East Midlands Area Conservative Women's Committee with special responsibility for three constituencies and as spokesman for One Nation Forum

1993 Invited to propose motion on Health at the National Women's Conference in London

1994 Organised national reception for Asian ladies to meet the Secretary of State for Health, the Rt Hon Mrs Virginia Bottomley JP MP. Invited to join the Blue Ribbon Committee by the Conservative Party.

Personal Interests

I enjoy reading, going to the theatre, cinema, cultural shows and attending medical conferences and seminars. I also enjoy travelling, keeping fit (trying) and swimming.

I love meeting people of different cultures and I enjoy entertaining them with my home-cooked foods. My husband's job as Commissioner for Racial Equality has enhanced this special interest.

Farzana Chowdhry

Fluent in *Urdu, English*

Religion *Muslim*

My Journey
I was born in Pakistan. I got a Masters degree in Zoology from the Punjab University. I worked for the *Pakistan Times* Publications for four years. I wrote four books on different social problems. These books are available in most British libraries.

My Life in Britain
I came to England after I married in March 1970. I worked in the Social Security Department or Income Support Section of the DSS for eight years. I gave up work in 1978 to look after my family. I was doing freelance work for various magazines.

Achievements & Contributions
I am Honourary Treasurer of Merton Racial Equality Council in Merton and Honourary Secretary of Millat Asian Housing Association. I am an executive member of the Asian Elderly in Merton and am in charge of the Donation Committee for All Pakistan Women's Association (APWA). I organise the Pakistani Business Women's Forum and also help various organisations in different ways as the need arises.

Personal Interests
I run a manufacturing company called SF Products in Cornwall Road in Sutton. I started the business in 1989 for fun. It worked very well. Now my company makes linesmen's flags, corner flags, golf flags, tabards, jackets, football suits, shirts and shorts. I have ten outworkers and two part-time workers.

My Journey

I was born in East Africa. My mother and father's families had emigrated to Tanzania many years previously. I spent the first seven years of my life in Tanzania. These were the formative years of my life. I was educated in a private American school and life was idyllic as a child in Tanzania. My father, being in the police force, enjoyed special privileges and we were brought up in a relaxed and carefree atmosphere. My mother was a headteacher in the Aga Khan School in Morogoro in Tanzania. My mother, brother and I came to England in 1967. My father followed a year later prior to national rule being implemented in Tanzania. My mother continued to teach in the UK for over 23 years.

Roohi Collins

Fluent in   *Urdu, English*

Religion   *Muslim*

My Life in Britain

We lived originally in Leicester, moving to Solihull in 1972 where my family lived in a predominantly English neighbourhood. I was one of only three Asians attending my school.

1967	Attended a junior school in Leicester
1970 – 1972	Attended Collegiate Girls Grammar School in Leicester
1972 – 1975	Attended Tudor Grange Grammar School in Solihull
1975 – 1977	Attended Sixth Form College in Solihull

1977 – 1980	Attended Birmingham University
1980 – 1981	Attended Chester College of Law
1982 – 1984	Qualified as a solicitor
1984 to date	Practising as a solicitor and partner

Achievements & Contributions

Combining a career with a family.

1980   Obtained LLB (Honours) upper second class at Birmingham University where I participated actively in several multi-racial organisations

1984   Joined my present firm as a solicitor

1988   Made a partner in my present firm and was the first Asian and female partner. I am also in charge of my department at the firm for the Leeds Office.

Personal Interests

I have a family of two young boys and another baby on the way, which keeps me fully busy when I am not working.

I enjoy living in the small village of East Keswick, Leeds where we mix with the local community.

I also play golf, as does my husband, and so we share a common interest which I hope my children will also share in due course. I like to travel, and try to keep fit as often as I can by undertaking aerobics and step.

I like to entertain and we have a wide range of friends from different backgrounds.

Dr Spinder Dhaliwal

Fluent in *Punjabi, English*

Religion *Sikh*

My Journey

I was born in India in 1964. I was brought up in a village in Jallundar until the age of three when I came to England. I have been in England ever since, although I have travelled widely around the world.

My Life in Britain

I have a BA (Hons) in Economics from Warwick University and a PhD in Financial Economics from Brunel University.

I am currently a Lecturer of Economics in the Business Studies Department at Roehampton Institute. I have worked in a number of academic institutions in the UK including Brunel University, Nottingham University and Kingston University. I contribute regularly to the *Asian Times* and consequently I am always on the look out for new material and interesting people.

Achievements & Contributions

In March 1989 I was invited to Tokyo University, Japan to present a paper on the UK financial system. This was funded by the Tokyo University and was an educational experience in terms of learning about the Japanese culture and economy. I am currently learning the Japanese language at evening class.

I have attended conferences in Germany, Portugal and Spain held by the European Economics Association of which I am a member. I have been to the US on several occasions to attend conferences.

I was a presenter of a current affairs/music programme for BBC Radio Nottingham. For this I received thorough training and developed skills in interviewing and radio journalism as well as mastering the technical side.

I was media co-ordinator for Apna Arts, a committee organising an annual nationwide open-air Asian festival. I was responsible for leading a team to help raise sponsorship money and to market the event to a nationwide audience. It was extremely successful and we got a good response from the BBC World Service, Radio France, Radio One's *Newsbeat* and the *Morning Star* to name a few. I am still involved with Apna Arts.

Personal Interests

On the sporting side I play squash and attend aerobics classes once a week. My work with the *Asian Times* enables me to meet many interesting people and attend a diverse range of cultural events. The media fascinates me and as well as radio and newspapers I have been in a number of TV shows such as *The Bill, Inspector Morse, The Good Guys* and *Between the Lines.*

Bilquis Durrani

Fluent in *Urdu, English, Persian, Arabic*

Religion *Muslim*

My Journey

I come from a deeply religious Muslim family of Central India. My father was a landowner, a Qazi and a supporter of women's education. We were six sisters and one brother. I had a happy childhood. Girls were usually educated at home. I was lucky to go to a single-sex school and college. I had a distinguished college career. I was in purdha until I got married. There are a few dates which stand out in my memory as beacons in my life.

1947 – The year the sub-continent of India was divided and Pakistan was created as the largest Muslim state on the map of the world. I was living in Delhi with my husband and little children. My husband was a Telecommunications Engineer in the Government of India. He opted for Pakistan. In September we came to Karachi after losing all our material belongings in the Delhi holocaust. We came to Pakistan with a determination and a will to make a new life there. By the grace of God we survived the agony of Partition and created for our children a happy and prosperous existence in Pakistan. My husband was selected by the UN as Telecom Expert and was sent to Oman (Jordan). I travelled with him all over the Middle East and lived in Libya for four years.

1972 – As my youngest son was studying in London we came here in 1972 from Libya and stayed on in Britain.

My Life in Britain

I joined various voluntary women's

organisations in Britain including the Islamic Party of Great Britain and National Federation of Women's Institutes. I was on the religious forum of Teddington School, Richmond. I have taken part in a discussion panel of the BBC on women's problems.

1984 – I founded the UK Women's Association for the Promotion of the Urdu Language. During that time there were hardly any women's organisations interested in the Urdu language. Urdu was not taught in schools. The women welcomed my Association with open arms and joined in earnest. To speak and hear one's language is a treat and a therapy and my Association offered this and a platform for those who could not attend men's functions. The Association is a member of the Merton Racial Equality Council and holds monthly executive committee meetings and functions, picnics and gatherings. It is a charitable organisation sending donations to deserving causes through Muslim Aid such as Bosnia, India, Sudan and Bangladesh. The membership is open to women and young girls of any cast, creed or religion who are interested in the Urdu language. All the meetings are held in the Open Door Community Centre, Beaumont Road, Southfields SW18.

Achievements & Contributions
Member of Karachi University Senate

Member of Board of Secondary Education, Karachi

Honourary Magistrate of Juvenile Court, Karachi

Lecturer in English at Central Government Girls College

Principal of Apwa Girls School, Karachi

Founder Principal of Khurshid Girls College, Karachi

Personal Interests
I write articles on topics of daily interest, especially for women. I speak on literary and religious topics. I read a lot of historical novels, biography and detective novels.

I love gardening; I collect exotic plants and visit the Chelsea Flower Show every year. I travel a lot and like to meet people of different cultures and learn about their customs. I listen to Radio Four and BBC World Service regularly. I relax in front of the TV in the evening while knitting.

Baroness Shreela Flather JP DL

Fluent in *Hindi, English*

Religion *None*

My Journey

I was born in Lahore when it was still part of British India. I left to come to Delhi during Partition. I went to school in Delhi and then to Isabella Thoburn College in Lucknow.

My Life in Britain

I came to England to study Law at University College London. During that time I met and married my husband and settled in the UK. When my two sons started going to school I started teaching.

Career Development

1965 – 1967   Infant teacher with ILEA

1968 – 1974   Teacher of English as a second language at Altwood Comprehensive School, Maidenhead

1974 – 1978   Teacher of English as a second language at Broadmoor Hospital

1976 – 1991   Councillor of the Royal Borough of Windsor and Maidenhead, being the first ethnic minority woman councillor when first elected.

1985 – 1986   Elected as Deputy Mayor

1986 – 1987   Elected as Mayor, being the first Asian woman mayor in the UK

I was Vice Chairman of the Estates and Amenities and Leisure Committees of the Royal Borough of Windsor and Maidenhead and secretary of the Conservative Group.

Achievements & Contributions

I was secretary/organiser of the Maidenhead Ladies' Asian Club from 1968 to 1978.

I started the new Star Boys' Club and summer school project for Asian children and prepared an English teaching scheme for Asian adults called 'Stepping Stone'.

My current appointments are as follows: Justice of the Peace since 1971; President of the Cambs, Chilterns and Thames Rent Assessment Panel since 1983; President of the League of Friends of Broadmoor Hospital since 1991; President of the Community Council for Berkshire since 1991; Governor of the Commonwealth Institute since 1993; Chairman for Tristar Broadcasting Ltd, the independent local radio station for the Windsor, Maidenhead and Slough area since 1992; Chairman of the Ethics Committee of Broadmoor Hospital since 1993; Chairman of a consortium of street children charities since 1992; Chairman of the Disasters Emergency Committee ; Vice Chairman of the Refugee Council since 1991; Director of Meridian Broadcasting since 1991; Trustee of the Hillingdon Hospital Trust since 1990; Trustee of Borlase School, Marlow since 1991; Trustee of the Rajiv Gandhi (UK) Foundation since 1993; Member of LWT Programme Advisory Board since 1990; Member of the Jewish Commission on Neo-Fascism in Western Europe since 1992; Member of the Management Committee Servite Houses; Member of the Council of the Winston Churchill Memorial Trust since 1993; Vice President of the Council of Atlantic College; Vice President of the Association of District Councils since 1990; Vice President of the Commonwealth Counties League since 1990; Vice President of the Association of Metropolitan Authorities since 1991; and Patron of the Cedar Centre, Isle of Dogs.

My Parliamentary appointments are as follows:
Member of the Select Committee on Medical Ethics from 1993 to 1994, Treasurer of the Indo-British Parliamentary Group; Member of the Executive Committee of the Penal Affairs Group; Member of the Executive Committee of the Population and Development Group; Member of the European Communities Committee from 1990 to 1993; Member of the Commonwealth Parliamentary Association; Member of the Inter-Parliamentary Union and Member of the British American Parliamentary Group.

I am now a Member of the House of Lords. I was raised to the peerage in June 1990, as a Conservative life peer.

Farzana Hakim

Fluent in *Hindi, Urdu, English*

Religion *Muslim*

My Journey

I was born in Paddington, West London, my parents having come over from India in the 1960s. Most of their brothers and sisters still live there. I have only been back a few times.

My Life in Britain

I became involved in Labour Party politics whilst a student at Stirling University. There I was elected to a number of positions including Women's Officer and Vice President of the Students' Union. This led to an involvement in the National Union of Students, firstly in Scotland and then in the UK as a whole. Following election onto their executive I took up a full-time post as the National Secretary of NUS in 1993. Throughout this time I was active as a Labour Party member and am now working with the Labour Party nationally as their Development Officer (Ethnic Minorities).

Achievements & Contributions

I have made various contributions to the national and local press, TV and radio, including Asian TV.

I have been an executive member of Central Scotland Racial Equality Council.

I was elected as the Vice Chairperson of the Scottish Anti-Racism Movement.

I have been involved in a number of campaigning initiatives for many years. This has included the organisation of various campaigns for representation at public events.

I have worked on various levels for the Labour Party at election time, including being an election agent.

Personal Interests

I am interested in politics at all levels. I enjoy taking part in political debate.

I swim regularly. I enjoy reading, particularly biographies and philosophy.

Nusrat Hameed

Fluent in *Urdu, English*

My Journey

I was born in Bhawal Nagar, Pakistan. My father was a food nutritionist in the army. I spent my childhood and early education in different countries due to my father's military duties. My later higher education was received in Rawalpindi up to the level of FA and I achieved a Bachelor of Arts Degree in Peshawar in 1959. I studied English, History, Philosophy and Urdu. I received prizes in English, Philosophy and Urdu. I participated in English essay writing competitions and wrote regularly for the college magazine. I participated in debates and was elected President of the debating society of my college.

My ambition was to be a lawyer, something unheard of for a woman in those days in Pakistan. I was able to gain admission to Law College in Lahore due to my debating achievements and good standard of degree. In order to support myself I managed to get a job as one of the élite team of receptionists at PIA Lahore Office. It was a demanding job from nine to five with evening shifts sometimes and regular further training courses. I found it impossible to continue my legal studies at the same time. I decided to save some money first and then complete my course.

Two years later in September 1962 I got married, having met my husband in the course of my job. I left my job at PIA and joined an American medical team researching the success of new contraceptive methods offered to the developing countries.

My Life in Britain

My husband and I came to the UK in 1964 because my husband wanted to complete a course in Air and Space Law. We decided to start a family and so I stayed at home until the children started school when I did accounts jobs in various offices, until the end of 1978.

I then decided to come back into education as I felt that with my qualifications I could do a better job. I found that I would need a Certificate in Education as my degree did not have the same official status as a UK degree. I applied for a grant in order to study for the Education Certificate but was told that grants were not given for the study of a second degree. Since I could not finance the course myself I had to give up the idea of teaching. I worked in a jointly-owned hardware shop with my brother.

I started taking an interest in community work. As I got in touch with other women in the Asian community, I realised they were in a desperate situation. Without any knowledge of English language, culture or their rights, they were confused and trapped, in poverty and ignorance. My own dissatisfaction was nothing compared to their plight. After the shop was sold in 1982, I was completely absorbed for about five years as the General Secretary of the Croydon Asian Women's Organisation. Some of the activities which I was responsible for included a drop-in centre for women, where women exchanged their ideas and skills, an exercise club, a youth club, a music class, information days on subjects such as education, health and housing, outings, concerts, fundraising activities, religious events.

I was also involved in the opening of a refuge for single Asian women. A playgroup for under fives and meetings for the elderly were also in the pipeline. A monthly magazine was produced. The organisation became a self-supporting, worthwhile body of active and capable women. I retired at the end of five years from active hard voluntary community work. I gained a lot of experience and insight working with various sections of the community and people from different backgrounds and walks of life. The knowledge of having been able to help others brought me a great sense of fulfilment.

In 1988 I began a three year part-time Diploma course in Homeopathy which I completed in September 1991. Soon afterwards I completed a short course in allergy testing using Vega Therapy. I started my private practice in 1991 as a homeopath. While homeopathy's popularity is increasing I feel there is a greater need for homeopathy for women.

Achievements & Contributions

I took up creative writing from 1976 to 1979 and wrote a women's column in the *Azad Weekly*, an Urdu publication in London. That gave me the opportunity to express the difficulties and problems Asian people were facing in this country.

Khalida Hashmi

Fluent in	*Urdu, Punjabi, English and I can read and understand Arabic*
Religion	*Muslim*

My Journey

I was born in India and my parents migrated to Pakistan during the revolution. I studied and was educated in Pakistan. I qualified as a doctor from medical school in Lahore and I served in the Missionary Hospital and then proceeded to England to learn further medicine in the UK.

My Life in Britain

To become a British registered doctor I had to take junior jobs in Scotland and learn the medicine of this country. I worked in the Psychiatric Departments in Birmingham and York. I also worked and learned Obstetrics and Gynaecology in various hospitals in London and acquired my diploma from the Royal College of Obstetrics and Gynaecology in London. I did my General Practitioner training in Woking, Surrey and became eligible to work as a GP in this country.

Personal Achievements & Contributions

At present I am working as a family GP in the south east of London. I feel I am serving the community of this area which is thickly populated with immigrants from abroad and I think I have a lot to contribute through my work. I have to advise and help the families in their needs for medical care and also in their requirements for housing and domestic grievances.

I voluntarily served with the Asian Women's Project in Woolwich.

I am serving at present on the British Medical Association for Lewisham as their Social Secretary, which I have done for the past three years.

I am, interestingly, taking part in the further development of this locality. I have attended medical meetings for the Meridian locality for further development.

I have been a member of the Anglo/Asian Society in the City of Westminster.

At present I contribute to the Night Medical Emergency Advice Service based in Acton, London.

Personal Interests

I have a keen interest in indoor plants. I am very fond of listening to music and I like to read and write poetry, in both English and Urdu.

Foqia Hayee

Fluent in *Urdu, English*

My Journey

I was educated at the Convent of Jesus and Mary School in Lahore, Pakistan and then attended the Government Intermediate College in Gulberg, Pakistan. In 1964 I received a Bachelor of Fine Arts Degree in Graphic Design and in 1968 a Master of Fine Arts Degree in Graphic Design at the University of Punjab in Lahore, Pakistan.

1968 – 1969   Full-time designer in MA Malik's Publicity Bureau in Pakistan

1969 – 1970   Full-time designer in Zinnia Graphics in Pakistan

1970 – 1972   Teacher at Crescent Model School in Pakistan

My Life in Britain

I worked as a part-time art teacher at Rochdale College of Adult Education.

1974 – 1976   Community Relations Officer for Rochdale Council for Racial Equality

From January to March 1975 I took a Course of Advanced Study, Assistant Community Relations Officer at Edge Hill College of Education.

1976 – 1979   Community Relations Officer for Greenwich Council for Racial Equality

From 1982	Teacher in ILEA primary schools
1986	Certificate in Language Teaching to Adults at Goldsmith's College, University of London
1986 – 1989	Teacher of Urdu to adults at Goldsmith's College, University of London

In 1992 I joined the Advisory Steering Group for the European Older Women's Project in Lewisham and realised how Asians were missing out on the projects developed by the council and had no say in the way their future was being shaped due to lack of knowledge and participation.

I set up an Asian People's Group and represented European Older Women's Projects in Medeira in Portugal in 1992, Perugia in Italy in 1993, Preston in Lancashire in 1993 and Denmark in 1994.

I was horrified to see the level of discrimination and lack of awareness of Black, Asian and other minority issues that exists in the rest of Europe. Britain is far ahead in this respect.

In May 1994 I was elected as a councillor and consequently as the first female Chair of the Pensioners' Committee in Lewisham. I also served on other committees including housing, transport, community sector, policy and resources and personnel.

I was elected as Mayor of Lewisham for the municipal year 1995 – 1996. I am involved in the democracy project, the Millennium working party and the quality commission for provision for the elderly. I take a keen interest in the Early Years sub-committee and an interest in finding ways to develop links between the young and old.

Personal Interests
My hobbies include Arabic calligraphy, stained glass, designing clothes, visiting and socialising with people from different communities and encouraging women to take an active role in society.

Radhika Howarth

Fluent in *Bengali, Hindi, Punjabi, English*

Religion *Hindu*

My Journey

I was born in Calcutta, India in 1963. My mother moved to Gwalior (Central India) and I started my education at the Scindia Public School, Gwalior.

I was very fortunate to get a good start in life by receiving education in this prestigious school. The focus here was not only on academic studies but also on extra-curricular activities which I think helped shape and develop my personality. Our motto in school was 'Satya mev Jayate' – 'Truth is always Triumphant'. I have always believed in this and it has given me immense strength and a way forward in life.

I graduated from Lady Irwin College, Delhi University followed by a postgraduate in Dietetics and Public Health and Nutrition. College education was as interesting and enjoyable as school. As a part of my studies I got an opportunity to work with organisations such as WHO, NIW, and UNICEF. My interest in social and community work started during my college life and I did a lot of voluntary work helping women and children.

My Life in Britain

I arrived in the UK in 1987.

1987 – 1992   Sales and marketing in a catering company

1992 to date   Project Co-ordinator of Age Concern for the Asian Carers Project

Achievements & Contributions

1989 Radio commercials for leading companies

1990 I set up my own small scale business designing and selling traditional Asian outfits. I organised fashion shows to promote the above and also to raise the profile of the rich culture and heritage of the Indian sub-continent.

1991 I joined the 'One World Action Group' as a volunteer. This is a London-based organisation providing aid and help to developing countries.
I got involved with market research. I am a consultant to a marketing company on marketing and shopping trends in the Asian community.
I set up Merton Academy of Dance and Drama.

1992 I did television commercials and was interviewed on satellite TV about issues concerning Asian women.
I joined two Housing Associations as a committee member.

1993 I joined the management committee of the Ethnic Minority Organisation in Merton.
I became a member of the Merton Volunteer Bureau and have joined their befriending scheme, providing help and support to an 83 year old housebound woman.

I gave various lectures and demonstrations about Asian culture and traditions in schools and libraries.
I helped in the fundraising for the Scanner Research Unit at St George's Hospital.
I am currently co-writing a book on healthy eating for the Asian community.

Personal Interests

I enjoy meeting people. I am a member of various women's groups; this gives me a chance to meet different people from a diverse ethnic background and make friends. I am particularly interested in Indian classical and folk dance. I get a great deal of joy and satisfaction helping the elderly and do this in my spare time.

Shahrukh Husain

Fluent in *Urdu and English, with some understanding of Punjabi, Gujarati, Marathi, Persian and Arabic*

Religion *Muslim*

My Journey

I was born in Karachi, Pakistan soon after Independence. I grew up to the sound of women's voices organising the country, giving me the feeling that women ran the world though often they allowed men to take the credit and appear in the front lines such as central government. I experienced a profoundly synthesised blend of cultural elements. In 1970 I went to Pakistan for the first adult franchise and was involved in organising my aunt's campaign to the National Assembly. I also ran a leading monthly, *Woman's World.* I was editor when I left at 21 for London.

My Life in Britain

1972 – 1973   Worked at a weekly tabloid, *The Competitor's Journal,* for about six months

1973 – 1976   Variety of freelance jobs, including publicity for film/TV companies

1976 – 1979   Honours degree in South Asian Studies with Arabic at the School of Oriental & African Studies (SOAS)

1979   M Phil in Modern Urdu Poetry at SOAS, upgraded to PhD in 1980

1980   Began work at the *Middle East Economic Digest* (MEED)

1981   Married and became pregnant one chapter away from completion of my PhD. Had my son in 1982 and continued work at MEED as Associate Editor, then Consultant.

Achievements & Contributions

I have produced three bilingual directories of the Middle East for Beacon Publishing, one of which won the Queen's Jubilee Award for Export. I also wrote a book on Urdu literature.

1985   I joined the British Board of Film Classification after a tough selection process and became a senior examiner there. I joined the South Asian Studies department at SOAS to teach Foreign Office diplomats Urdu and culture before they went out to Pakistan.

1986   I had a children's book called *Focus on India* published.

1987   Completed a children's book called *Exploring Indian Food* and edited Floella Benjamin's book on West Indian food in the same series. I taught Urdu for SOAS External Services Department. Students included MPs, careers advisors, local politicians, members of the DTI and people involved with television and film.

1989   I wrote the script of Anita Desai's screenplay adaptation of her novel *In Custody*. I also translated and co-edited a number of BBC documentaries including *Ashes and Dust*, produced and directed by Michael York. This won several awards.

During 1991 and 1992, I gave several seminars on subjects relating to Indian cinema, Indo-Anglian women writers and the experience of displacement and immigration. I continued to contribute to anthologies and encyclopedias on my specialities: folklore, film and Urdu poetry. I also acquired a certificate in Psychodynamic Psychotherapy. I was commissioned by the Newham Drug Prevention Through Puppet Theatre to write an anti-drugs play. I researched and wrote *A Megawicked Story* which has been a great success with schoolchildren. In 1993, I was a judge on the broadcast of the Ghazal competition. I began work as a psychotherapist. *Mecca*, my new children's book was published and well received. I edited and introduced the *Virago Book of Witches*. I also helped edit the rough cut of *In Custody* in New York. This was selected for the London Film Festival.

1994   I rewrote a screenplay for the Walt Disney Picture Company, which is currently in pre-production.

Personal Interests

I am a bit of a recluse and love reading, time spent with my family, 1960s pop-folk music, Indian classical music and folklore of the world. I enjoy living in London. I have friends from diverse social, cultural and racial backgrounds. I like cooking for friends and sharing views with people.

My Journey

I was born in Dar-es-Salaam, Tanzania. My parents came to East Africa from Lahore, Pakistan (then India). I spent 24 years in Tanzania and was educated at the Government Secondary School. I then went to Highridge Teachers Training College in Nairobi, Kenya.

Life in East Africa was very enjoyable and interesting without any pressures or political tensions. I left Dar-es-Salaam in 1961 and settled in Leicester.

My Life in Britain

My teacher training course in Highridge, Nairobi was accepted and I started teaching in Leicester in September 1961.

Parveen Ibadulla

Fluent in	*Urdu, Punjabi, Hindi, Gujarati, Swahili, English*

Religion	*Muslim*

Career Development

1961 – 1968	Taught at Medway Junior School, Leicester
1969 – 1971	Taught at Overdale Junior School, Leicester
1974 – 1991	Taught at Abbey Primary School, Leicester

I took early retirement in 1991 but still do some supply work.

Achievements & Contributions

To my knowledge I was the first Asian teacher in Leicester in 1961. I was a pioneer of teaching English as a second language in 1962 because this was part of my training as a teacher.

I was responsible for Religious Education at my last primary school. I also contributed towards Religious Education courses by giving talks on 'Insight into Islam', Muslim festivals and religion in the home of a Muslim family.

I was responsible for multicultural education at the same school. I produced a booklet called *Festivals* along with Mr Gulab Mistry (Deputy Head at the school). It has information about Christian, Hindu, Sikh, Muslim, Chinese and Buddhist festivals along with suggested classroom activities and follow-up work for the children.

Since taking early retirement from teaching, I have learnt to swim and have been doing a lot of community work and organising various activities. I am on the management committees of the following organisations:

British Diabetic Association; Leicester Asian Youth Association (LAYA); Society for Intercultural Understanding (SICUL), which promotes deeper understanding of different faiths and cultures by having outside speakers and organising special festival and cultural evenings; Asian Sports and Cultural Centre (ASCC), which promotes cultural awareness and encourages sports of all kinds to youngsters; Leicester Asian Ladies' Circle, which raises funds for at least three charities a year; Federation of Muslim Organisations (Women's Section), which organises seminars on religious, health and other issues that affect women; and the Muslim Ladies' Association.

I also started a drama group with Asian ladies who had no previous experience of acting or going on a stage. They successfully took part in a play and performed it in front of the audience of 200 women. The play was in Urdu and was written, produced and directed by me.

Personal Interests
I enjoy travelling, swimming, walking, acting, socialising and meeting people of all races and backgrounds.

Gulshan Jamani

Fluent in *Gujarati, Hindi, Urdu, Swahili, Kutchi, English*

Religion *Ismaili Muslim*

My Journey

I was born in East Africa. My father left India sometime after 1900 to set up a printing press business in Tanzania and Uganda. I spent 30 years in East Africa. During this time I was educated at the Government School up to secondary standard ('A' levels) and then joined Kenya Commercial College for a diploma course in Business Studies.

I later enrolled at the Makerere University College to take extra-mural classes in English Literature and subsequently took up Maria Montessouri Method of Education in teaching infants.

During my married life, apart from taking care of my family, a husband who was practising as a GP in medicine, two children and my job as a Montessouri teacher, I was very involved in voluntary social services. I have been on the executive committees of various respective organisations, such as Uganda Council of Women (Secretary then Chairperson); YWCA (Sub-committee Chairperson); Save the Children Fund (Member Executive); Family Planning Association (Executive Committee); President's Appeal Fund on Poverty, Ignorance and Disease; Mayor's Charity Ball Committee; Aga Khan Provincial Council's Tribunal Committee and other societies. It was very enriching working with the higher authorities of multilingual and cultural societies on community programmes. Although this demanded a lot of time and energy, it gave me great pleasure and satisfaction in serving the local community.

My Life in Britain

Throughout my working life in Britain I have enjoyed being a part of helping to raise funds for the needy. At present I am concentrating on children, and on women of the world projects for Third World countries.

Achievements & Contributions

1956   Invited to a garden party at the Governor's House in honour of Her Majesty Queen Elizabeth II and the Duke of Edinburgh at Entebbe, Uganda

1968   Received certificate on a good job done on President's Appeal Fund on Poverty, Ignorance and Disease, by the President of Uganda, Dr Milton Obote

1969   Invited by the Mayor of Uganda to serve on his Charity Ball Committee

1973   Nominated as a Chairperson by the Brighton Asian Circle in Brighton

1983   Invited to join the Lioness Club (Host) Westminster Branch in London on the Board of Governors

Personal Interests

I enjoy meeting people. My hobby is singing Indian semi-classicals. I love cooking (when I am in the mood). I am a self-employed person and my interest lies in the current market. Last but not least, I love socialising.

Prabha Jassal

Fluent in *Hindi, Urdu, Punjabi, English*

Religion *Hindu*

My Journey
I was born in Nairobi, Kenya as was my mother. My father and my mother's ancestors came from Sargodha which is now part of Pakistan. My childhood memories of Nairobi are of freedom, laughter and a lot of open space.

My Life in Britain
I came to England when I was ten to begin my secondary education, I then went to a teacher training college to fulfil my ambition of working with children. My teaching career began in Enfield. I married in 1975 and moved to Kent. I have two children, my daughter Sonia who is 14 and attends the Dartford Grammar School for Girls and my son Samir who attends Riverview Junior School. After many successful years of teaching I am now a headteacher at Greenleaf Primary School in the London Borough of Waltham Forest.

Career Development

1973 – 1975   Teacher at Southbury Junior School, Enfield where my probationary career was completed. I taught seven to nine year olds and arranged a PE club as an extra-curricular activity.

1975 – 1985   Teacher at Lawn Road CP School at Northfleet in Kent. I taught six to eleven year olds. I ran a successful netball team and initiated a science resource area with guidelines for approaching science for five to eleven year olds. Extra-curricular activities were netball, drama and swimming clubs.

1982 – 1989   Teacher at Whitehill Junior School at Gravesend in Kent. I taught eight to ten year olds. I ran two successful netball teams. I was responsible for computer studies and topic work (Incentive A) from 1985 to 1989. Extra-curricular activities were drama, swimming, athletics, netball and needlework clubs.

1989 – 1991   Deputy Headteacher, Science Co-ordinator, Staff Development Co-ordinator and Appraisal Co-ordinator at Elaine Avenue CP School

1992 to date   Headteacher at Greenleaf Primary School

I have played an active part in all aspects of school environment and have endeavoured to develop myself professionally by attending courses in all curriculum areas, including special educational needs provision and multicultural education. I have attended many courses on Management in Education.

Achievements & Contributions

1973 to date   Attended in-service residential and day courses in all curricular areas to keep up to date with current practice

1984 – 1991   Organised self-help groups for parents to address issues related to children's education

1987 – 1989   Committee member of Ethnic Minority Teachers' Group.
Completed a Diploma in Primary School Management.

1989 – 1990   Completed a Certificate in Managing Primary Schools

May 1993   Speaker at Conference on Bilingual Children's Education

Personal Interests

I enjoy living in Kent where there is a feeling of openness and space. I enjoy walking, reading, playing squash and swimming. A lot of my time away from work is spent in activities which involve my children.

Mercy Dhushyanthi Jeyasingham

Fluent in *English, some Tamil*

Religion *Christian*

My Journey

I was born in Sri Lanka into a Tamil, Christian family. When I was two years old my parents emigrated to Britain with myself and my older sister. I grew up in South London in an inner city environment in the early 1960s. This is where my observation of racism and deprivation occurred.

I attended local schools. My parents believed strongly in education (my mother was a teacher) and so both my sister and I obtained science degrees at university. My sister went on to obtain a doctorate. After I had started full-time work I studied and gained an MSc in Interprofessional Health and Welfare studies. Although I was brought up to be proud of my heritage we rarely spoke Tamil at home and in those days there was a very small Tamil community in Britain, therefore I do not speak Tamil fluently.

My Life in Britain

As I spent some years getting the qualifications I needed to enter university (I attended Aberdeen University) I entered the job market late and at first found it difficult to get a job. I studied marketing at night school and during the day did voluntary work for my local Community Relations Council, learning about structural and institutional racism across housing, employment and education and investigating racial harassment cases.

My first paid job was working in administration in Camden Council's

Planning Department. I quickly moved on to work for a Westminster disability charity and set up the first disability information and welfare rights service based in a London hospital (St Mary's, Paddington). I then became National Development Officer on Black Health for the National Community Health Resource (NCHR). This national charity was involved in supporting community development and health work in local communities. At NCHR I organised many national conferences and seminars on Black and minority ethnic health, covering subjects such as mental health, women's health and the health of refugees. I ran a national network (the Black Health Forum) of individual workers and organisations concerned with inequalities in health in communities. I was also involved in a number of advisory groups, committees and working parties.

I now work for Hammersmith and Fulham Social Services Department as Head of Care Standards. My section sets quality standards across all in-house services by carrying out in-depth quality audits involving users, staff and advocacy organisations.

Achievements & Contributions

I have worked with a number of different organisations including the Health Education Authority, the King's Fund Centre for Health Service Policy, the Greater London Association of Community Health Councils and the National Children's Bureau. I have been on the management committee of organisations such as the UK Health for All Network and the London Community Care Alliance. Currently serve on the Health Education Authority's advisory group on Sickle Cell and Thalassaemia, and the community care resource group of the NHS management executive's Ethnic Health Unit.

I am a director of the Unity Initiative charity (set up to support teachers and youth workers combating organised fascism). My main voluntary work, however, is as part of an organisation called Minorities into the 21st Century (C21) which promotes the value of cultural diversity. We have organised a number of conferences on subjects such as human rights in Britain and political participation in multicultural Britain (jointly organised with the All Party Committee on Race and Community). We are also involved in cross-party lobbying on race and religion. I have been invited by the Home Office to participate in a number of race relations seminars.

Personal Interests

My paid work and voluntary work keep me quite busy but I do get a chance to relax with friends and family. My mother loves travelling and as she is blind I get to go along too – time and money permitting! I have also been involved for the last couple of years in a number of self-development education programmes that I have found very beneficial.

Sujata Jolly

Fluent in *Hindi, Punjabi, Swahili, English*

Religion *Hindu*

My Journey

I was brought up in Kenya where I studied up to 'O' levels. My reminiscences of my childhood are of sport, fun, study and the freedom to develop a career for myself.

I moved to India in 1965 for higher education, opting for medical sciences. I had a passion for learning through experimentation which at times brought me into conflict with the traditional teaching of science subjects in India where the emphasis was on memorising rather than learning.

I married Parmod Jolly, a successful scientist, in 1968 and came to the UK the same year for permanent settlement.

My Life in Britain

My career started in the research laboratories of ICI and blossomed with other similar major organisations. I seized all opportunities of further education to help my career and, most importantly, achieve my objective of specialising in cosmetology. I used my knowledge and experience in formulating treatments for colleagues and friends with skin disorders.

My career progressed smoothly in a very happy family environment receiving constant support and encouragement from my husband and two daughters, Sapna and Superna.

1982 was a momentous year for me I left the cosy world of employment for the challenging life of self-employment. I started my own company, Dépèche Mode Laboratories, with the company motto of 'Simplitas, Probitas, Integritas'.

Achievements & Contributions
The development of successful treatments for a wide spectrum of skin problems. These treatments are available in beauty clinics both in the UK and abroad. These treatments are also recommended by some surgeons and dermatologists.

The introduction of Hi-Lines, the art of permanent make-up in the UK.

The publication of articles on skin problems in consumer and professional magazines.

Participation in forums discussing skin problems on radio and television. I am actively involved in a campaign against skin-lightening products mainly used by Afro/Asian women. I also help local authorities in their efforts to educate the ethnic population against the dangers of using skin-lightening preparations.

I have lectured on the development of products and treatments for skin problems in professional meetings in the UK and abroad (Iceland, Norway, Cyprus, Jersey, Greece, Brazil and Singapore).

I have lectured at various women's group meetings on skin problems.

Personal Interests
I enjoy music and classical dancing. I paint for relaxation and I have held two exhibitions of my work in Maidenhead. My work takes me to different parts of the globe where I always find time to learn about the local cuisine. I occasionally swim and play tennis.

Nimmi Joshi

Fluent in *Hindi, Urdu, Punjabi, English*

Religion *Hindu*

My Journey

I was born in Punjab, one of three sisters and three brothers, growing up in Ambala. I studied at the University of Punjab, gaining a BSc (Hons) in Science and an MSc in Zoology. I was also a lecturer in Zoology at the university. I was awarded a scholarship to do a PhD by the University Grants Commission of India but, having completed one year's research study, I left India to take up teaching in Canada.

After graduating as a teacher from the University of Manitoba I took up an appointment as a High School teacher in Winnipeg, working with 'problem' children. I also entered into community work, specialising in the care of elderly people. In addition, whilst working in Canada, I gained experience as a broadcaster on regular local radio programmes.

My Life in Britain

I came to England with my husband, Ashok, in 1974 and was immediately absorbed into the broadcasting and media world, as a pioneer of the nascent commercial radio sector in Britain. I have two sons, both born in the United Kingdom, Deepak (1978) and Rishi (1983).

Career Development

1975 Came to the UK at the start of independent local radio. Engaged in scriptwriting and voice-overs in commercials, for the first Asian programme, *Geet Mala* on BRMB Radio in Birmingham/Midlands.

1977   Scriptwriting and voice-over for *Geet Mala* on LBC Radio (London area).

1978   Presenter for *Jhankar* on Beacon Radio (Wolverhampton and West Midlands). Continued presenting for more than ten years. This programme was much revered as a 'friend of the family' by the listeners.

1983   Presenter of the first *Asianwide* programme to be heard throughout the UK and Europe on Radio Luxembourg.

I also presented *Sangeet Sarita*, as well as the programme of the same name, on Mercia Sound in Coventry and the *Subrus* programme on Radio 210 in Reading.

All these programmes won popular acclaim as feats of excellence among the Asian media. The regular *Asian Topic* phone-in was also hailed for its achievements in helping to break down the barriers between the Asian and indigenous listeners to Beacon Radio.

Since 1990 I have produced and presented *Eastern Buzz* on Buzz FM in Birmingham; a pot-pourri of music, news and views, 'talkback' phone-ins, guest and celebrities. I have also presented Radio Harmony in Coventry, specialising in Asian topics and problems.

Achievements & Contributions
1982   Midlands Co-op Award for Beacon Topic

1983   ALVA Award – Best Presenter

1984   ALVA Award – Best Presenter and Best Linguist

1985   ALVA Award – Best Presenter

1993   Invited to serve as Executive Member of National Organisation of Asian Businesses

Screen playwright, scriptwriter, lyricist and linguist in Asian languages. Member of British Actors' Equity Association. Executive member of the National Organisation of Asian Business.

Personal Interests
Cooking (wrote LBC Radio Cookery Book), presentations, drama, acting, music, PR and entertaining friends.

Mahmuda Kabir

Fluent in *Bengali, Hindi, Urdu, English*

Religion *Muslim*

My Journey

I was born in Dhaka, Bangladesh. My parents migrated to what was then East Bengal from the Birbhum district of West Bengal. I spent all my life in Dhaka and was educated there. I graduated and completed a Masters degree from Dhaka University.

I grew up during the period when Bengali people were fighting to preserve their rights to speak mother tongue which led to the creation of the new country of Bangladesh. My political career actually started then. As a university student I was involved in political activities for the freedom of language.

I came to Britain in 1966 with my husband, Dr H Kabir, to complete a post-graduate degree with a British Council Merit Scholarship. Sweet memories of Bangladesh have never been erased from my mind and never will be. I was a social welfare organiser in Dhaka on the Directorate of Social Welfare before coming to Britain.

My Life in Britain

My first stop in Britain was in Edinburgh. We stayed there for about a year then we moved to Glasgow. I completed my MSc, PhD and CQSW at Glasgow University from 1968 to 1974.

Career Development

1967   Social worker (Glasgow)

1968 – 1974   Studying for the above
              mentioned degrees and

had two children during this period

1974 – 1980   Social worker (Glasgow)

1980 to date   Senior social worker in London

I am at present Team Manager in Southwark Social Services Department.

Achievements & Contributions

Up until 1980 I was bringing up my two sons and had little opportunity to be involved in public life. I have achieved my goal as my eldest son Jahangir is now a doctor and my second son Alamgir is a fourth year medical student. I consider that is one of my greatest achievements, to bring up two sons successfully in a foreign country.

1980   Became an active member of a political party

1983   Elected by the people of Lewisham as a representative to the Education Consultative Committee for Ethnic Minorities in the ILEA.
My name was published in the *Asian Who's Who* reference book and is still included.

1984   Joint secretary of Lewisham and Kent Islamic Society and Treasurer of the Bangladesh Women's Association in the UK

1985   Joint secretary of the Asian Forum

1986   Selected to become a member of the Police Consultative Committee

1988   Set up the South East Bangladesh Women's Association in Lewisham

1990   Elected as a Labour Councillor for London Borough of Lewisham. I was interviewed by the BBC world and overseas services.

1992   Received a special invitation from Buckingham Palace to have lunch with Her Majesty the Queen and Heads of the Commonwealth countries in the Commonwealth Institute.
Received award from a Bangladeshi newspaper as a successful Bangladeshi woman.

1992   Elected Vice-Chairperson of Race Relations Committee of ALA.

1994   Received 'Coat of Arms' award for notable service to the community. My name has been placed on the Parliamentary Candidate List for election as an MP.

Personal Interests

My main interest is politics. I enjoy the constructive debates in politics. I like to travel; in 1992 I travelled all over Europe. I enjoy driving, reading biographies, the theatre and socialising. I would like to work for the benefit of underachieving children in education and the welfare of women.

Gulzar Kanji HMI

Fluent in	Hindi, Urdu, Gujarati, Kutchi, English
Religion	Ismaili Muslim

My Journey

I was born in 1941 and schooled in Dodoma, Tanzania. My father was a primary school headmaster. I attended Makerere University, Kampala from 1959 to 1964 and received an Honours degree in English.

My Life in Britain – Career Development

I came to Britain in 1964. I worked as a supply teacher in primary schools in London. I took my teacher training at Maria Grey College, Twickenham.

1965 – 1966	Teacher in primary schools in Surrey
1966 – 1970	Teacher in primary schools in Cambridge
1970 – 1976	Teacher in primary schools in Haringey
1976 – 1978	Deputy Headteacher at Muswell Hill Infants, Haringey.
1978 – 1984	Headteacher at Campsbourne Infants, Haringey
1984 – 1990	Inspector for bilingual education; District Inspector for early years; Staff Inspector and then Senior Staff Inspector (overseeing some 800 primary schools) until ILEA abolished
1980 – 1985	External examiner at

	Walsall College of Higher Education
1981 – 1985	Consultant in education at Aberystwyth University
1985 – 1989	Member of Steering Committee of Schools Council National Oracy Project. Member of working party set up by the National Curriculum Council to produce policy document on multicultural aspects in the National Curriculum.
1990 to date	HMI (Her Majesty's Inspector of Schools) only female Asian HMI.

Professional Development

University of London Institute of Education – Diploma in Role of Language in Education

Goldsmith's College, University of London – Advanced Certificate in Early Childhood Education

Achievements & Contributions

I was married in 1964 to Nizar Kanji, formerly a barrister, now a solicitor in private practice in West London. We had one daughter, Yasmin, who died in 1992, aged 27.

I have written articles and book reviews and lectured in primary education and management. I am a member of the Gujarati Literary Academy Examination Committee. I visited Delhi as guest of the Government of India and toured Gujarat as guest of Gujarat Government 1984. I am active in Ismaili Community Education Research Committee.

I have counselled innumerable teachers and others in Education.

Personal Interests

English and Gujarati literature, poetry and gardening.

As a civil servant I cannot now write articles or reviews, lecture or undertake consultancy work – paid or unpaid – outside the remit of OFSTED work.

Lily Khan OBE, MA, BT, DIP ED

Fluent in *English, Bengali, Urdu, Arabic, Hindi*

Religion *Muslim*

My Journey

I was born and brought up in Baghdad, Iraq. I attended the American School for Girls in Baghdad, St Francis Xavier's School in Dhaka, Scottish Church College in Calcutta, the American University of Beirut in Lebanon, Harvard University in USA and Teacher Training College in Dhaka. My teaching experience was from 1950 to 1971. I worked as a teacher in schools in Dhaka, Rawalpindi and Nawshera, West Pakistan. I worked as a headmistress at two schools in East Pakistan and was principal at two further schools in East Pakistan and Khulna.

My Life in Britain

I am the widow of the late Major Shauket Ali Khan. I have two daughters and nine grandchildren.

Member of Childcare for the Save the Children Fund.

Advisory Committee member on Asian programmes for the BBC.

Commissioner on the Commission for Racial Equality.

Co-ordinator of the Homeless Families Project (Westminster and Camden)

Director of the Asian Studies Centre, Tower Hamlets

Lecturer in English as a Second Language and tutor of English for immigrants, Tower Hamlets

Member of the committee which compiled the Burnage Report on Racism in Manchester schools.

Twice took part in compiling surveys of Bangladeshis in Loughborough.

I am currently on the Advisory Committee for the Save the Children Fund. I am General Secretary for the Merton Asian Women's Group and a member of the Asian Elderly Group of Merton, the Commonwealth Institute, the Bangladesh Centre in Notting Hill Gate, the Bangladesh Bhavon in Islington and MVSC in Merton. At the present time I am the Chairperson for the Ethnic Minority Centre in Mitcham. I was elected to that post in 1991 and was re-elected in 1993.

Achievements & Contributions

I was awarded a gold medal and a citation for services to Education in 1968 (Decade of Development in Pakistan). I met Mr Jennah (the then Governor General of Pakistan) representing the students of East Pakistan. I took an active part in the 'Language Movement' in East Pakistan. I founded and organised and am still connected with several women's groups in Bangladesh. I was Chairperson of the Asian Women's Community Workers Group (home for battered women in Southwark and Lambeth).

I have written short stories for adult English language learners and am the author of *Bangladesh Information Handbook* and the co-author of *Murder in the School Yard*. I have given lectures and completed courses for different authorities all over the country. I often give talks to different groups including teachers, social workers, community workers, the police and the prison service. I work actively with refugees. I have been invited to Buckingham Palace on three occasions. I participated in the Victoria and Albert Project – 2nd phase in 1993.

I have visited many countries for conferences, seminars and as a representative of different educational and social bodies including USA, Germany, Italy, Egypt, Syria, Jordan, Lebanon, India, Pakistan, Thailand, Malaysia, Singapore, Saudi Arabia, Kuwait, Canada, Hong Kong, China, Iraq, Iran, Belgium, Holland, France and Ireland. I was a delegate to the United Nations in New York.

Personal Interests

I enjoy social and community work, travelling, knitting, tapestry, patchwork, painting and music.

Saroj Lal

Fluent in *Hindi, Punjabi, English*

Religion *Hindu*

My Journey

I was born in Gujranwala in what is now Pakistan and at the time of Partition my family moved to India, which gave me the experience of being a refugee in another country. My childhood was influenced by my father's involvement in the fight for independence for India, and his ideas about democracy and women's rights. I was educated in Chandigarh where I completed an MA in Economics in 1962 and I taught for a few months in Ludhiana before getting married.

My husband was working in Madras where I stayed for three years, after which I moved to Singapore where he had been offered a teaching position. Since we were expatriate staff, I was not allowed to work and this gave me a compulsory rest while bringing up my son who was born there. Singapore gave me the experience of living in a multi-racial society and from there I came to Birmingham where my husband was taking a postgraduate degree. So I moved from Pakistan to India, to Singapore and then to England where I encountered racism for the first time. I eventually settled in Edinburgh where my daughter was born.

My Life in Britain

In Britain I continued my education by doing a teacher's training course at Moray House, but that was at a time when there were no crèche facilities so bringing up a family came into conflict with my career.

1969 – 1970   Moray House College of Education

1970 – 1973	Primary School Teacher, Morningside Primary School
1973 – 1976	Voluntary work with the Women's International Centre (YWCA)
1976 – 1980	Community Worker with the YWCA Roundabout International Centre
1980 to date	Lothian Racial Equality Council, first as a Community Relations Officer and now as Director (first black woman Director in Scotland)

Achievements & Contributions

Working with the LREC has meant involvement in race and equal opportunity issues in a wide range of areas. My involvement has given me an opportunity to press for race equality for black and minority communities through representation on and negotiation with various bodies in both the private and public sector: race relations sub-committees, Lothian and Borders Police, Lothian Health Board and trusts, the Social Work Department, Multicultural Education Advisory Group of the Education Department and other black and ethnic minority organisations in the voluntary sector working in the race relations field.

Personal Interests

My job leaves me little time for personal interests, since it is such a demanding and stressful – and occasionally frustrating – one. Given time I would like to enjoy my home more and to travel. I enjoy travelling and I have recently been to Japan and the USA for the first time.

Pinky Lilani

Fluent in *Hindi, English*

Religion *Muslim*

My Journey

I was born in Calcutta, the city of joy and one of enormous culture. I was educated at a convent run by Irish nuns and then took my degree in Education, graduating from Calcutta University. My postgraduate qualification was in Social Communication Media from Bombay University with a thesis in Public Relations. Among the many activities I dabbled in were fundraising for the World Wildlife Fund, appearing occasionally on TV and comparing a radio programme. My last assignment before being swept off my feet by my prospective husband was with a magazine.

My Life in Britain

Arriving in London in the late 1970s after getting married was very much a time for integration and adaptation. After having my children I returned to study part-time on my postgraduate Diploma in Management Studies.

In 1988 after graduating I began lecturing in Croydon. Living in Britain exposed me to a wide variety of people from all over the world and enabled me to pursue many different interests from politics to the arts.

Career Development

1988 Diploma in Management Studies and Diploma in Marketing

1993 Certificate in Education (FE)

1994 Advisor and assessor for the National Vocational Qualification

1994 to date   Master of Education
                degree

Part-time lecturer in management, marketing, interpersonal development and cookery.

Achievements & Contributions

I am a consultant to a large manufacturing company for new product developments in Indian food. The company supplies seven large UK supermarkets.

I set up my own company 'Development Dynamics' which runs classes for companies on interpersonal skills and management subjects.

I was very actively involved in fundraising for the United Nations Development Fund for women (committee member) and Women Aid. I helped with the Women of the World Lunch and several balls.

In 1990 I was Chairperson for 'Walk for a Cause' to raise money for the Aga Khan Foundation, the British Heart Foundation and the National Deaf Children's Society.

In 1992 I was Chairperson for the Arts for the Ismaili community. I organised the first Arts Day with Fay Weldon as the chief guest.

Since 1993 I have been a member of the National Council of His Highness the Aga Khan for UK and Europe.

Personal Interests

My passion is meeting people and observing interpersonal dynamics. I am evangelical about helping people develop themselves. I also enjoy entertaining, cookery and visiting restaurants. The world of theatre, cinema and the arts are areas which, in spite of enjoying, I am never able to have enough of. I like to think of myself as an enthusiastic, productive and energetic person.

Sudershana K Mahindru

Fluent in *Hindi, Urdu, Punjabi, Gujarati, English*

Religion *Hindu*

My Journey

I was born in Gujranwalla, which was then in India, on 24th April 1939. My parents, who originally migrated from Lahore, settled in Tanzania. I come from a large family with nine brothers and two sisters! My parents worked very hard to bring us up. There has always been a strong bond between family members.

I did my secondary education in Tanzania and later worked at the Veterinary Services for two years to contribute financially towards the upbringing of my brothers and sisters. I have always loved teaching so I took a two year professional course at Dar-es-Salaam Teacher Training College from January 1960 to December 1961. I got married in 1965.

My Life in Britain

Unfortunately, my teaching qualifications were not recognised in Britain. This was very frustrating because, having settled in Britain after marriage, I did not want to pursue any other career except teaching in a primary school. Therefore I decided to add a few more 'O' levels and 'A' levels to my qualifications. I had no choice except to study at home because I was bringing up three young children under five. Through sheer determination and resolution I got through my 'O' levels and 'A' levels.

In 1973 I joined the teacher training course at Birmingham Polytechnic. I took English as my main subject and Drama as a subsidiary subject. I helped my community by interpreting at weekends at Dudley Road Hospital for those ladies who could not understand English.

Achievements & Contributions

1976 – 1985   Worked as a primary schoolteacher in an infant school with special responsibility for Drama and Multicultural Activities

1986 – 1987   Successfully completed BEd (Hons) degree in Multicultural Education on full secondment from Birmingham LEA

I took a one-year evening course in Child Drama (Diploma in Child Drama). In January 1988 I was promoted to Scale Three as a Home School Liaison Teacher. I gave two direct language lessons at West Hill College. I gave a talk at the Language Centre on Multicultural Activities to some primary schoolteachers and, from time to time, gave talks on 'Teaching through Mother Tongue' at the Multicultural Support Services. I taught English to the newly-arrived children from India and Pakistan in 1976 (one term only) on a voluntary basis. It helped me a great deal to gain insight into children with social deprivation and its influence on education. I wrote a curriculum for a multicultural society for my school.

Personal Interests

I'm afraid my personal interests have changed with age. I used to love cycling, yachting, dancing, singing, music, films, reading and cooking. I wanted to learn to play piano but, unfortunately, I could not afford the fees. Now I still pursue some interests like reading, singing, music and swimming and I watch my favourite plays on the TV. Unfortunately I was struck with arthritis in the knees. I had a total knee replacement in 1988 of my left knee. I am waiting for my right knee to be operated on this year (1995). Hopefully, God willing, I shall be able to do my MA in Education. I strongly feel that the more I study the more ignorant I feel so that my journey of academic pursuits is still incomplete!

Surryia Mahmood

Fluent in *Hindi, Urdu, Punjabi, Spanish, English*

Religion *Muslim*

My Journey

I was born in Punjab, Pakistan. My grandfather had moved to Rawalpindi in the latter part of the last century. I graduated from Punjab University and was trained as a teacher by the Froebelion Missionary Institute in Murree, Pakistan and postgraduated from Peshawar University.

Being the first daughter after five sons I enjoyed life being special without any discrimination at home. I remember life was full of freedom of thought and speech. Before coming to the UK I was teaching in an International School at Tarbela Dam, Pakistan. Spending eight years in the company of 17 nationalities in a small place like Tarbela was very enriching in many aspects.

I came to live in Britain in 1977 and learnt that my qualifications are not recognised and 12 years of teaching experience was not enough to be a qualified teacher in England.

My Life in Britain

1977 – 1978   Teacher of English as a Second Language at the Earl Marshal Adult Education Centre, Sheffield.

1978 – 1979   Area organiser for English Language Scheme for the Education Department in London Borough of Croydon

1983 – 1985   Playgroup leader

including a course for 'Helping the Handicapped Child in the Playgroup'. Voluntary work at various playgroups.

1985 onwards Secondary School Teacher in London

From 1987 to 1989 I was seconded to work on Urdu language as a Project Officer for Graded Assessment in Modern Languages Scheme. I successfully completed the GAML Scheme of Urdu which was accepted by the School's Examination and Assessment Council as complementary to the GCSE examination. This is the only published assessment material for Urdu language which is graded into different levels and is nearest to the prescribed levels of languages within the National Curriculum.

Achievements & Contributions

1978	Series of lectures at the Workers' Educational Association, Rotherham
1979 – 1985	Volunteer for Croydon Asian Social Services
1988	Accorded qualified teacher status
1990	Invited to join the committee looking into the National Curriculum of Community Languages
1991	Course of Spanish for

teachers in Wandsworth and was successful in GCSE examination

1992	Attended two short courses of Spanish language at Madrid University
1993	Invited by Spectrum Radio to contribute to their educational programme
1987 – 1990	Invited to contribute to the presentations at the exhibition of ILEA and also at All England Conference in Manchester in 1987

I have organised various INSETs and workshops for community language teachers, multicultural education and bilingualism including teaching of modern and community languages.

Personal Interests

I like meeting people from different cultures. I have a wide circle of friends from many different ethnic groups. Languages fascinate me and I enjoy learning and teaching the languages I know. I love music and regularly attend an Indian music class in Norbury. I have a special interest in community work.

Adeeba Malik

Fluent in *Punjabi, English*

Religion *Muslim*

My Journey

I was born in Bradford in the late 1960s after my parents arrived from Lahore, Pakistan as part of the mass migration of prospective textile workers. The eldest of four children, I went to local state schools where I thoroughly enjoyed and cherished schooling from the age of five to 18. I left school with sound qualifications and went to Humberside College where I received a 2:1 in my Bachelor of Education (Honours) degree.

I consider myself very fortunate in 'my journey' as it has always been interesting, exciting and somewhat unpredictable. Being a young Asian woman I feel I have a lot to contribute to society as a whole and hope that people, in particular women, can benefit and learn from my experiences.

My Life in Britain

1991 – 1992	Middle school teacher and co-ordinator for Religious Education
1992 to date	Language and Training Development Manager

Achievements & Contributions

1985	Head girl of a large inner city upper school
1988 – 1990	Student representative at Humberside College of Higher Education
1991	Co-ordinator of Religious Education

Featured as a 'role model' for an educational careers video *Positive Images* for young people nationally

1992   Joined an inner city development agency QED (Quest for Education and Development)

Developed a successful and unique language training programme for unemployed minority ethnic communities of Bradford

1994   Main speaker for the National Women's Register Conference attended by 600 people on 'Are We Really a Multicultural Society?'

Member of the Special Needs Review Committee for Bradford and District Training and Enterprise Council

Director of EASA (Education Advice Services for Adults) in Bradford, a voluntary organisation

Award winner for 'Yorkshire Young Achiever Award for Education and Training'

Member of the international group for women 'The Soroptimists'

Personal Interests

My work! My work is a hobby – it aims to improve the economic circumstances of minority communities in Bradford. I enjoy socialising, travelling and good food.

Zahida P Manzoor

Fluent in *Urdu, Punjabi, English*

My Journey

I was born in Rawalpindi, Pakistan and came to England at the age of four. My father was a retired Army officer.

My Life in Britain

I commenced nursing training at West Suffolk General Hospital in January 1977 and after obtaining my SRN qualification became a Staff Nurse at the same hospital. I then moved to Birmingham where I obtained my Midwifery qualifications and went on to qualify as a Health Visitor at the University of Leeds. I worked as a Health Visitor in the Durham area for a year before returning to Leeds. Having obtained a teaching certificate in my own time, I then spent a approximately two years lecturing in Health Education to BTec students, followed by 18 months as Deputy Head of Department for a Women's Institute in Saudi Arabia.

On return to England, I completed a full-time Applied Social Studies Masters Degree course at the University of Bradford and at the end of the course was offered the post of Youth and Community Education Officer with Bradford Metropolitan District Council.

Soon afterwards, I was asked to take on the role of North East Programme Director for the Common Purpose Educational Trust, a charitable organisation responsible for establishing new networks and looking at different ways of promoting cities such as Bradford.

My appointment as a non-executive Director on the Board of the Bradford Hospitals NHS Trust brought me back into the NHS and in December 1992 I was appointed Chairman of the Bradford Health Authority. I am currently Chairman of the Shadow Board of Bradford Health Commission formed in anticipation of the merger of Bradford Health Authority and Bradford Family Health Services Authority in April 1990.

Achievements & Contributions

1991 – 1993	Governor, Sheffield Hallam University
1992 – 1993	Governor, Bradford and Airedale College of Health
1992	Winner of the Yorkshire Business and Personality Award
Since 1992	Member of the Council of the University of Bradford

Since 1993 I have been a director of Bradford City Congress (a forum of business and public service leaders committed to improving and promoting the image of Bradford); a director of Bradford City Challenge Ltd; and a Commissioner for the Commission for Racial Equality.

I am a member of the National Corporate Governance Task Group set up by the Secretary of State to look into issues around open governance in the NHS; a member of the National Advisory Group set up by the National Association of Health Authorities and Trusts to look at Health Authority mergers and commissioning and the Chairman of a Joint Working Party of NAHAT and the King's Fund Centre which looked at Board membership within the NHS in relation to ethnic minorities. The NAHAT report was launched in November 1993 by Baroness Cumberledge.

I have chaired and spoken at various national conferences on health and ethnic minority issues. I have a fundraising involvement with several local charities.

Personal Interests

I enjoy living in Bradford. There is an excellent theatre and the award-winning National Museum of Photography, Film and Television. It is also within easy reach of the Yorkshire Dales National Park.

I enjoy collecting antiques, particularly furniture and rugs. I am very interested in architecture and I am delighted that so many old buildings are being successfully renovated, although it is disappointing that a great many have also been lost. I am married to Dr Madassar Manzoor. We have two children – Nadia, aged nine and Sara, aged three.

Sheila Markanday

Fluent in *Hindi, Gujarati, English*

Religion *Hindu*

My Journey

I was born in Kenya. I received training in Indian Classical vocal music from Professor Rajopadhye and Khansahib Ghulam Mustafa Khan who are leading exponents of the Gwalior style of vocal music teaching in Bombay.

My sitar training was conducted by Khansahib Abdul Haleem Jaffer, a very accomplished sitar player in India. I regularly gave performances on stage, radio and television in Nairobi and was very well known throughout East Africa. I started giving music lessons on the radio in Nairobi and this people found very educational and entertaining.

At the Kenya Music Festival where they had entries of Indian songs, dance and instrumental music, I was invited to adjudicate their items and I personally donated trophies to the Festival Committees and also handed trophies to many young talents.

My Life in Britain

London is now my permanent place of abode and I conduct music classes for all age groups. I have performed for BBC radio and my recent debut on BBC 1 on the *Afternoon Plus* programme where I rendered sitar melodies was well enjoyed by the viewers. Toronto television took the opportunity of my visit there and interviewed me on one of their programmes and also recorded several of my songs for future programmes.

I have also given several stage performances in some well-recognised halls, including the Royal Albert Hall, Royal Festival Hall, Wigmore Hall and Logan Hall.

My recent concerts in Dubai and Dublin were very successful. I have also given sitar concerts in other parts of Britain and abroad.

A new role as composer and music director for an Indian film shot in Bombay and London with popular Indian film stars has given me further incentive.

Achievements & Contributions

The teaching and performing of music, both vocal and instrumental. I have tried to propagate Indian classical music in this part of the world and in East Africa where I established a successful school of Indian music for both vocal and instrumental music.

My proudest performance was for Prince Edward. I played sitar for the prince and for the high officials of the British regiment.

Personal Interests

Music, cooking, gardening and travelling.

Jamila Massey

Fluent in	Hindi, Urdu, Punjabi, German, English
Religion	Christian

My Journey
I was born in Simla, North India, and have lived in Britain since 1946 when my father became a producer for the BBC Eastern Service. I have a degree in English, Latin and Urdu from King's College, London.

My Life in Britain
My first BBC broadcast was made in 1947. I have since broadcast in Urdu, English and German. The first film I acted in was *Sink the Bismark*. I have appeared as a running character in several comedy series and soaps in addition to straight drama.

I have worked in many films and played a variety of characters on stage.

Achievements & Contributions
I have co-authored a novel and books on Indian classical music and dance with my husband Reginald Massey.

I was for many years a member of the Afro-Asian Committee of Equity, the actors' union, and the first woman to chair it. Personally it gives me great satisfaction to see that the early hard work of the Afro-Asian Committee is now bearing fruit and new young Asian actors and actresses are now getting a somewhat fairer bite of the cherry.

Personal Interests
I read voraciously and enjoy gardening, tapestry, sewing, wine making and jam making. Apart from this I love to try and get away with merder (sic) when playing scrabble with my son Marcus.

Dr Lata Malviya McWatt

Fluent in *Hindi, Urdu, English*

My Journey

I was born and brought up in Allahabad, India. I was educated at local primary and Government secondary schools. I graduated from the University of Allahabad in 1967 and became a lecturer at the University (1969 – 1971). In 1971 I won a post graduate scholarship at the Queen's University of Belfast to research on social/urban structure of Indian cities.

My Life in Britain

1971 – 1974	Postgraduate research, the Queen's University of Belfast, Northern Ireland – awarded a PhD
1974 – 1975	Lecturer, University of Allahabad, India
1976 – 1988	Worked for the Commission for Racial Equality in various capacities. Worked mainly in Formal Investigations, Research (Commission funded).
1988 to date	Policy Adviser (Community Relations) London Borough of Croydon

Achievements & Contributions

1986 – 1987	Played a major role in helping to set up the Urban Trust, now based in Birmingham.
1983 – 1988	Played a significant role as part of the team in a number of the Commission's formal investigations and research projects.
1988 to date	As Croydon's Policy Adviser, have helped the Council in bringing about major changes with regard to Equal Opportunities issues.

Currently I am the Chairperson of the Council's Refugees' Working Party.

I am closely involved in health and community care issues in Croydon and have represented on various Health/ Community Care committees.

Personal Interests

I enjoy going to theatres, art galleries and museums. I like to travel around the world – I have travelled around a lot. I love going to concerts. I enjoy painting, particularly water-colours. In my spare time I also do a lot of reading.

Faryal Mirza

My Journey
I was born and brought up in London.

My Life in Britain
At James Allen's Girls' School I gained ten GCSEs and three 'A' levels in French, German and English Literature. In October 1993 I took up a place at St Hilda's College, Oxford University to read French and German.

My parents have always stressed the importance of education in their children's lives and I cannot emphasise how great their influence has been on me. My mother and father have always encouraged my intellectual and creative development, as has my grandmother. They also taught me how to maintain my cultural heritage and at the same time integrate into British society.

Achievements & Contributions
I write poetry, mostly in English, and I started writing at around nine years old. I have had a collection published, *One Second Dream*, and some of my work has appeared in periodicals both here and in Bangladesh.

I have taken two poetry writing courses at the Arvon Foundation Centre in Devon. The first time I was invited by the National Poetry Society to attend their workshop, the second was with a school party. Both were amazing experiences which proved extremely beneficial to my writing. I continue to write poetry and have read my work at numerous functions. I have also begun to explore other creative avenues such as fiction.

I am interested in drama. I have been awarded certificates in Speech and Drama and I also have a GCSE in Dramatic Arts. At James Allen's Girls' School I directed the Sixth Form play which was an exhilarating experience which I hope to do again. I have also compered at a number of social events which was tremendously enjoyable and something I hope to repeat.

I want to continue with my writing and I wish to pursue a career in law or the media which would enable me to use my creative skills.

Personal Interests
I enjoy writing and also travelling. I have visited myriad countries. I find travelling a wonderful way of opening the confines of narrow minds and I also like meeting people from different cultures.

Nuzhat Mona Mirza

Fluent in *Urdu, English*

Religion *Muslim*

My Journey

I was born in 1974 in Birmingham, England. My parents are originally from India but they migrated to Pakistan after Partition.

In 1980 my parents and I settled in Pakistan. My mother opened a school, which she ran successfully until 1983. Due to circumstances we returned to London and settled back into life in Britain.

I gained fluency in Urdu during my three years in Pakistan. Since our return to Britain in 1983, we have continued to make regular visits to Pakistan.

My Life in Britain

1977 – 1980	Honeybourne School in Birmingham
1980 – 1983	Schooling in Rawalpindi, Pakistan
1983 – 1986	Argyle Primary School in London
1986 – 1991	Walthamstow School for Girls in London for my secondary education
1991 – 1993	Ealing Tertiary College in London

Achievements & Contributions

1985	As part of a class project we persuaded the Council to build a safe playground for children living in the King's Cross area
1986 – 1991	Actively took part in plays at school as well as attending Drama Club
1990	My first article was published in The National Union of Teacher's magazine, during my two-week work placement
August 1992	Worked for four weeks in Karachi for *She* magazine
February 1993	Worked on a voluntary basis for a homeless organisation in Acton
March 1993	Began working at *The Daily Awaz*, a daily newspaper where I had a few features published
August 1993 to date	Working at TV Asia as a researcher

Personal Interests

For me, the field of media is not just an occupational interest, but a personal interest as well. My job as a researcher at TV Asia, requires me to enjoy my work completely, as our work does not finish once we have left the studio. Whether we are at home or at a social function, we are constantly looking for suitable guests for our programmes.

Parween Mirza

Fluent in	*Urdu, English*
Religion	*Muslim*

My Journey

I was born in Naushera Peshawar, in Pakistan. My parents migrated to Karachi where they settled. At the age of five I joined the Children's Club at Radio Pakistan, Karachi. I wrote my first story at the age of eleven which was published in a monthly children's magazine.

I was educated at St Joseph's Convent School, I then went on to do my BA at the Government College for Women in Karachi where I was an active member of the dramatic society. I continued my work with Radio Pakistan until 1970 when I got married and left Pakistan to settle in England.

My Life in Britain

I joined the BBC World Service, as soon as I came here and worked there on a casual basis for the last 22 years.

1977 – 1987   Joined BBC Television presenting both Gharbar and Naye Zindagi Naya Jeevan which later changed to *Asian Magazine*.

1990 – 1992   Joined Sunrise Radio as a Presenter/Producer. I worked with them for two years doing a variety of programmes including a mini drama series which ran daily for three months. I did a programme for the holy month of Ramadan called *Waqt E Sehr*.

1992 – 1993	Joined a marketing company as their Media Marketing Manager which was a job created especially for me. I did radio programmes for them and handled all their advertising, promoting their various products.

Achievements & Contributions

1983	Major role in *Shaam Dhaley Savera*, an Urdu play which was staged at the Commonwealth Institute, London
1984 –	Appeared in *Qubool Qiya Main Ne* (I Do I Do) at the Shaw Theatre, London
1986 –	Large role in *The Great Moghul* staged during India Week
1988 – 1989	Honourary Tutor for a Drama Course for young people in Britain run by Palm Pride Ltd
Sept 1989	Lead part in a play called *Baja Irshad* which was staged by the Hyderabad Deccan Association
May 1992	Worked with the Access Broadcasting Company on their trial radio for a month presenting a variety of programmes
Nov 1992	Invited by Channel Four to appear as a judge on their Ghazal Competition which was aired in December and January

I have been a member of a variety of associations related to poetry over the years that I have been in England and have met many famous poets and writers. I have also written articles for Urdu newspapers like *The Daily Jang* and *The Daily Awaaz* about women's issues and short stories. My articles have appeared in Urdu magazines such as *Shafaq* and *Shama,* both of which are monthly journals.

Personal Interests

I enjoy living in Wembley, which has a large multicultural population of Asians. I enjoy socialising and most of my friends have a love of Urdu poetry and Urdu literature like myself which makes socialising fun. My main interests are broadcasting, poetry and Urdu literature.

Shaukat Mirza

Fluent in *Urdu, Hindi, English*

Religion *Muslim*

My Journey

I was born in Fatehgarh UP India. I was educated at Government Girls' Primary/ Secondary School where I passed the Matriculation Examination in 1958. I migrated to Pakistan with my parents in the same year. I passed my MA Degree in Social Work obtaining 1st Division from the University of Karachi in 1967.

I found the city of Karachi a place of opportunities and freedom where women were seen in all fields of employment. This new environment encouraged my determination to be an independent and professional woman.

My Life in Britain – Career Development

1968 – 1974	Social Worker in the Midlands – working with old and physically handicapped people and also with families and children
1975 – 1976	Postgraduate Certificate in Education from Birmingham University
1976 – 1978	Employed by the Adult Education Department at Lozells in Birmingham where I taught English as a Second Language
1978 – 1980	Community worker for a church organisation in Birmingham
1980 – 1983	Headteacher in a primary school in Islamabad
1983 to date	I have gained a senior position in my school. I am an Early Years Co-ordinator and have responsibility for Science and Design/ Technology

Achievements & Contributions

I have always been involved in working with Asian organisations and helped them in promoting our culture and language. I have been chairperson for two organisations – the Muslim Ladies Circle in Leyton (1989 – 1992) and the Asian Children's Link in Walthamstow (1987 – 1989). At present, I run a group called the Asian Women Writers' Circle where multilingual poetry sessions are held.

Due to my personal interest in children I wrote a book of Urdu poetry for young children which was published in 1990.

Young children have not only been a strong part of my career development but have also been close to me personally. In Karachi I voluntarily spent much of my time with children in remand homes and orphanages. In England my close link with children has been through organising and running playgroups.

Personal Interests

I write Urdu poetry and enjoy attending Urdu poetry symposiums where I read my poetry and listen to other poets. I enjoy listening to semi-classical Asian music and ghazals.

I play the keyboard in my spare time. I also enjoy reading.

Dr Aruna Nath MB, BS, FRCOG, FFPM, RCP(UK)

Fluent in *Hindi, Urdu, Punjabi, English*

Religion *Hindu*

My Journey

I was born in 1942 in Lahore, India. I do not remember much of my life there as I was less than five years old when Partition in 1947 brought my parents, myself and my younger brother to Simla. I studied in St Thomas School there till the age of 17 when we moved to Delhi as a part of my father's secondments to various government appointments. In Delhi I joined Lady Irwin School to finish my secondary education, joined Hindu College to do my pre-medical studies and finished my medical training at Lady Hardinge Medical College.

I had a fairly happy childhood and remember enjoying taking part in dramatics, musical events and excursion tours in school and college life. I am married and have two sons and one daughter. I have been resident in the UK since 1966.

My Life in Britain

Worked in various hospitals in London including:

1966 – 1967	British Hospital (BHMB)
1968 – 1969	King's College Hospital
1970 – 1972	Registrar in Gynaecology, Westminster Group of Hospitals
1973	Research Assistant, St Bartholomew's Hospital Medical College, London
1974 – 1980	Senior Registrar and

	Medical Officer of Council for Investigation of Fertility Control
1980 – 1982	Medical Officer, Redhill General Hospital, Surrey and also Principal General Practice at Beckenham, Kent and Consultant to Wembley Hospital, Middlesex
1982 – 1990	Medical Officer Medicine Dn DHSS
1990 to date	Senior Assessment Consultant, Medicines Control Agency, Department of Health.

Since 1970 I have been the Instructing Medical Officer – Family Planning and Joint Committee on Contraception. My memberships include Fellow RSM, RCOG, Faculty of Pharmaceutical Medicine RCP, Blair Bell Research Society, MSSVD, NAFPD, Medical Women's Federation, ODA, IMA, IPMS.

Achievements & Contributions

I have had various medical articles published including 'The Problem of Cervical Smears', *Family Planning*, 1974. I am a member of various social, cultural, religious and charitable societies including Bhartiya Vidya Bhaven (life member), Hare Krishna Movement, Hindu Centre, Hindu Society, Asian Women's Association, South London Indian Council, India Association Southern Branch, and am the Chairperson of South London Satya Sai Organisation, UK.

I have served as Professional Secretariat on committees on 'Review of Medicines', 'Dental and Surgical Materials', 'Medicines Commission', 'Safety of Medicines'.

From 1989 to 1993 I was Chairperson of the National Women's Forum of the Overseas Doctors' Association in UK. I was a member of Croydon Council's Forum with interest in health and social security issues. I am a past vice-chairperson of the South London Indian Council and chairperson of the Elderly Day Centre, Croydon. I was a School Governor at the Applegarth School, Addington, Croydon. I lectured at the Society of Intellectuals in Covent Garden on 'Hinduism and its Association with other Religions in SE Asia': an example of successful blending of career, family responsibilities, interest in religion and devotion to social work.

I have been included in the *World Who's Who of Women – Twelfth Edition*, and *International Who's Who of Contemporary Achievement – Third Edition*. I have won several awards including Hind Rattan (1991), International Woman's (1992), Woman of the Year (1993).

Personal Interests

Music, reading, comparative study of religions.

Sharadaben Patel

My Journey

I was born in India and educated at a boarding school which followed high ideals of work and encouraged interest in religion, culture and social understanding. The school also followed a strict programme of healthy pursuits which began at 4 am with physical exercise, yoga, meditation and breathing exercises.

I left boarding school at the age of 16 to travel with my parents to Africa where I continued my education up to 'O' level standard. Both my parents were influential in my development. In particular my father, who was a headmaster, believed in education for boys and girls. I was fortunate that in my father's house I was actively encouraged to be involved in community activities. This started with girl guides, culture programme and women's religious groups. It gave me enormous satisfaction to help the community. I was in the first group of voluntary workers to work in family planning from 1964 to 1966. I ran a religious, social and physical group from 1955 to 1967. Six years after the untimely death of my husband, wishing to give my children the benefit of university education in England, I left Africa in 1967.

My Life in Britain

After the early few years in England I started my voluntary work in helping people in a small way by taking the needy to hospital, to the doctors, shopping and to religious ceremonies. Some groups were started in South London by Social

Services and I took the opportunity. In the beginning I used to go to Eldon Hall and then got a place in Norbury Methodist Church Hall. Here I started with the help of a team of four ladies. The main activities were Acupressure or Reflexology which helped people in pain where traditional medicine had not helped, reading of scripture books, sewing, knitting and singing. Our group gave the normally housebound and isolated Asian ladies a sense of going out to learn more about themselves and their adopted country. For many it was the first time in their lives that they had been swimming and played games. We held a very successful Reflexology Seminar in Oswal Mahajanvadi for four days.

1965 – 1975	Member of Hindu Centre, North London and worked as a committee member. Founder member of Arya Samaj in Ealing.
1980 – 1986	Member of the Caribbean Hindu Society where I taught Hindi language and demonstrated cookery
1980 to date	Served on the Committee for One World Week
1981 – 1985	Member of Elderly Support Group and Aassyana Project on the South London Indian Corporation
1985 to date	Chairperson of Jagruti Asian Women's Group

I was a founder member of Croydon Asian Women's Organisation and a committee member of the National Association of Patidar Samaj.

Achievements & Contributions

1975 to date	Worked as an interpreter/helper for Social Services, Hospital Service, GPs, DHSS Housing
1981 – 1984	Mother tongue classes. Voluntary work for religious ceremonies and funeral services, any money received being donated to charity.
1992 – 1993	Took part in making a video for the Department of Health on the Menopause, Fitness and Exercise and was thanked by Baroness Comberledge
1993	Jagruti Group was awarded the London Borough of Croydon's first Community Award. I was chosen as one of the four individual voluntary community award finalists in the above scheme.

Personal Interests

My personal ambitions are to help people and I will continue doing my voluntary work as long as I am able.

Huma Price

Fluent in *Hindi, Urdu, Punjabi*

Religion *Muslim*

My Journey

I was born in Lahore, Pakistan. My father came to Britain soon after I was born. I completed all my primary education in Pakistan. My mother and I came to Britain when I was eleven years old. Upon our arrival, we discovered that my father was living with a woman and had no intentions of re-establishing our family. Due to her lack of formal English education my mother became dependent on me to survive in an unfamiliar environment. My father's rejection of us left me saddled with the responsibilities of an adult at the tender age of eleven. An unbelievably hard struggle followed for me, resulting in a lost adolescence and an incredibly hard early adulthood.

Despite these setbacks I tried to make a success of my life. I decided to become a barrister. I had no emotional or financial support from anyone. I worked in the evenings and studied during the day. I believed that my struggles had come to an end when I was finally called to the Bar in 1991, only to discover that it was virtually impossible to find a pupillage, primarily due to the recession.

On a more personal level, I finally feel settled in my life. The stability, love and affection I craved from my father never came. However, the man I have married has made up for all my sufferings and provided more love than I imagined existed.

My Life in Britain

1971 – 1977   Secondary School, 'O' and 'A' levels

1981 – 1982	Certificate in Youth and Community work
1983 – 1987	LLB (Hons)
1987 – 1988	Certificate in Teaching English
1990 – 1991	Bar Finals
1992 – 1993	Certificate in Psychology Certificate in Counselling

From 1981 to 1983 I was a youth and community worker/counsellor. I developed work with young women which included organising schemes for their education, training and advancement. I was also responsible for counselling them for their general welfare.

Since 1983 I have taught English as a second language to a variety of students in various schools and colleges across London. I have also taught Urdu occasionally.

Achievements & Contributions

1985 – 1986	Member of the Academic Board advising on the planning, co-ordination, development and regulation of the academic work of various educational institutions
1987 – 1990	Management Committee of Battersea and Wandsworth Law Centre

1991 – 1992	Radio broadcaster hosting discussion and entertainment programmes for Britannia Radio, a local community station. Acted as a Press Officer, liaising with the press for reviews/publicity of plays produced by Awaaz Theatre Company, based in South London.
1990 – 1993	Freelance writer. I am currently writing a book on Family Law.

I am in the process of setting up a women's group called the Eastern Women's Association.

Personal Interests

I enjoy fashion design and dressmaking. I have organised several fashion shows. I like reading in both English and Urdu, particularly Urdu poetry. I am an active member of Urdu literary associations such as Urdu Markaz and Bazme Urdu. I also have an interest in Urdu music and have arranged several concerts with visiting singers and musicians from India and Pakistan. I like travelling and meeting people from different cultures.

Kailash Puri

Fluent in *Punjabi, Hindi, Urdu, English*

Religion *Sikh*

My Journey

I was born in Pothodar, Rawalpindi (now Islamabad, capital of Pakistan). My family moved to Lahore. I was educated in Kallar (our village), Rawalpindi, Lahore and Lucknow. I came to England in September 1946 to join my husband who was a Research Fellow, working for his second doctorate in Ecology and returned to divided India in 1948 with our nine month old son. We lived in New Forest, Dehradun, Poona, Allahabad, spent a few years at the University of Ibadan, Nigeria and the University of Science and Technology, Kumasi, Ghana. I presented the Woman's Hour weekly programme on WNTV Kumasi for six months.

My Life in Britain

1966 – 1967   Editor *Kirna Weekly*, Southall

1966 – 1968   Civil Service in Harrow Land Registry

1966 – 1968   Punjabi teaching to Police Officers, Health Visitors, Nurses and Doctors. Once a week Indian Cookery in an Adult Education Centre in Southall

Achievements & Contributions

1968   Chairperson of the United Nations Association. Participated in BBC TV Asian Programmes (Sunday mornings).

1968 – 1972   Merseyside Community Relations Council

1968 – 1978	Chief Editor of *Roopvati*, a women's monthly magazine
1972 – 1975	Consultant (Indian food) Marks & Spencer
1975	Started Crosby Yoga Centre and established East-West Family Advisory Circle
1975 – 1989	Visiting Lecturer at Leith School of Food and Wine
1976	Invited by Director of Education to look into the problems of Asian schoolchildren
1981	Invited by LBC Radio to do an Agony Aunt/ Counselling phone-in for Asian listeners
1984	President, UK Asian Women's Association
1988 – 1992	Governor of Woodlands School, Formby. Invited to address Oxford University Students' Union.
1992	Vice President, Women's Society for Peace and Friendship (London)
1993 to date	Agony Aunt for TV Asia, every Tuesday morning

I have been featured in the *Sunday Times Magazine* and *Mail on Sunday Magazine*. I presented numerous papers to international conferences including: Trans-cultural Psychiatry Conference in Bradford in 1975; International Conference on Unity of Sciences in Seoul (Korea), Tokyo and Kyoto in 1980; International Cultural Foundation Conference in Cairo in 1983; British Academy of World Peace Conferences in London, Edinburgh and Leeds Castle, Kent in 1983 – 84; a paper on 'Asian Women's Position in Society' in Southall in 1980; Assembly of World Religions in New Jersey and Barry Town, USA in 1985; International Punjabi Conference at the GN University, Amritsar in 1991 and London in 1993; Empowerment of Women (ICUS) Conference in Seoul (Korea) in 1992.

I have received numerous awards including 'Woman of the Year' from the North West Literary Circle, Bhai Mohan Singh Vaid Literary Award, Tarn Taran, Arba-be-Zoke Poetry Award (Merseyside), Prerna Literary Award (Delhi), Shiromani Sahitkar Award, Patiala, Shiromani Award, Institute of Sikh Studies, Delhi and 'Personality of the Year' from Khalsa College, London. I am the author of 28 books.

Personal Interests
Indoor plants, Indian music, Chinese, Continental and North Indian cooking, flower arrangements and the company of interesting people.

Talat Qureishi

Fluent in *Urdu, English*

Religion *Muslim*

My Journey

I was born in Poona in India. I arrived in the UK at the tender age of four. I am one of five girls in my family. I believe that without the support, encouragement and total belief our parents had in our abilities we would not have attained our successes.

My Life in Britain

1986 Journalist for *International Indian Film Magazine*

1987 Joined Nationwide Building Society

1989 Promoted to first Branch Manager position Finchley Central

1990 Promoted to Branch Manager, Golders Green

1991 Promoted to Branch Manager, Kingston

1992 Head-hunted by senior management to Marketing Division to represent the entire branch network in the UK

1993 Returned to Kingston Branch

1994 Requested by senior management to develop and manage the Customer Service Manager in East Surrey region.

1995 Returned to Kingston Branch

Achievements & Contributions

Elected President of the Asian Building Society at Kingston University. Passed all professional examinations, CBSI within two years.

Completed postgraduate qualification whilst in full-time employment!

Won several junior tennis titles and represented Merton in the school tennis league as well as hockey and netball.

Selected to appear in the *Working in the Money Business* magazine.

Personal Interests

I am a very keen tennis player and enjoy most sports. My intentions to keep fit and healthy resulted in my taking up aerobics and yoga.

I enjoy visiting and exploring different countries and cultures. I feel privileged to have visited many parts of the globe. Whenever possible I try to visit the theatre, ballet and art galleries.

Good food, good company and a lively discussion is another favourite pastime.

Yasmin Qureshi

Fluent in *Punjabi, Urdu, English*

Religion *Muslim (Sunni)*

My Journey

I came to the UK in 1972 with my family as a child from Pakistan. I went to school in Watford.

My Life in Britain

My parents were not fluent in the English language. However, they encouraged my sister and myself in the educational sphere. My sister is also a barrister. Whilst my sister (who is a year or so older than me) and I were studying, a lot of Pakistani and other Asian people would ask us to read, translate and write letters on their behalf to councils, DSS, immigration authorities and so on.

Achievements & Contributions

BA (Hons) in Law
Bar at Law
Masters in Law

Governor of West Herts College

Governor of Laurance Hains JMI

Member of Southall Rights Centre (I work as a volunteer for them)

Was a member of the Free Representation Unit

Secretary of Watford Constituency Labour Party between 1989 and 1991

Chairperson of Watford and District Fabian Society between 1991 and 1992

Personal Interests

I have been very actively involved in the Labour Party in Watford. This has involved canvassing, leafleting, publishing newsletters and so on. Apart from my activity in the Labour Party, I have been doing a lot of other voluntary work within the community. My hobbies are aerobics, reading and fencing.

Yasmin Qureshi

Fluent in	Urdu, Hindi, Punjabi, English

Religion	Muslim

My Journey

I was born in Lahore, Pakistan. My father was from UP and was a member of the Pakistan Hockey Team after Partition. He played in the 1952 Olympics, held in Helsinki, Finland.

I completed my schooling in no less than ten schools in different cities of Pakistan as my father was constantly transferred due to his job in the Civil Service. I used to take a keen interest in drama and music and was a scholarship holder during my entire education. I won 'best girl of the year' award at Multan, stood second in Multan division in Metric exams and was head girl for two years.

I suppose travelling and living in different parts of Pakistan has enriched and broadened my outlook. I completed my degree in Biology from Lahore College for Women, during which I got married and came to England.

My Life in Britain

The first few years of my life in Britain were totally dedicated to my family. I had three children in quick succession. During that time I stayed in touch with the world beyond by taking up recreational classes.

Career Development

1983 – 1984	Modelled for portrait classes
1986 – 1987	Modelled for Indian fashion shows
1988 – 1993	Comparing for charities and at ladies' association functions
1990 – 1991	Vice-President of the North London Association for Muslim Women, 'Khawateen'
1990	Joined Sunrise Radio, participating in different radio programmes
1992 – 1994	Participated in comedy drama serials for the BBC World Service
1992 to date	Worked for TV Asia as a news presenter

Personal Interests

I enjoy travelling, music, meeting interesting people and reading, especially on meditation, human psychology and relations, health, nutrition and biographies. I have a wide circle of friends from many different ethnic groups. I enjoy yoga and have attended regular classes for nine years. I am also interested in interior designing, fashion and cooking.

Surangani Ranasinha

Fluent in *Sinhala, English*

Religion *Buddhist*

My Journey

I was born and educated in Sri Lanka. After graduating in English and Philosophy, I accompanied my doctor husband who came over to Britain for postgraduate studies.

I recall my childhood in Sri Lanka as a happy one. I enjoyed the security of an extended family. Life was full of freedom with no political tensions. I grew up in a truly harmonious multiracial/ multicultural society – so different to what exists today in Sri Lanka.

My Life in Britain

1963	Started my career as a primary teacher in ILEA
1968	Went back to Sri Lanka with my son and daughter when my husband joined the University as a Lecturer in Medicine. I did some voluntary teaching of English as a second language to socially disadvantaged children.
1971	Returned to UK due to political unrest in Sri Lanka to educate my son and two daughters
1971 – 1991	Continued as mainstream primary teacher in Merton. Postholder for Special Educational Needs and responsibility for the Child Protection Team.

1992 to date	Bilingual Teacher (Team Leader of Bilingual Assistants) in Early Years Bilingual Project in Merton

Personal Contributions

In 1964 I joined the Buddhist Women's Association and I am involved in many activities of the London Buddhist Vihara in Chiswick where my husband is the principal of the children's Buddhist Sunday School.

I have been involved in family contribution for TV and radio programmes on Buddhism and have provided whole-school INSETS on Buddhism in Primary Schools.

I helped to organise the teaching of Sinhala language classes in Merton.

I was involved in raising charity funds for third world countries. I then took a Counselling Course at Westminster Pastoral Foundation and undertook voluntary counselling of ethnic minority families who have problems with children growing up in two cultures.

Followed a three year course of Psychotherapeutic Counselling at Tavistock Institute of Marital Studies in London and found this experience invaluable in talking to the increasing number of Asian couples who approach Relate and other voluntary services with marital problems.

Personal Interests

I live in a quiet and friendly neighbourhood in Epsom. I enjoy painting and wood carving. I love going to the theatre. I also enjoy Kandyan dancing and continue to attend Yoga classes, an interest I have pursued for a number of years.

My Journey

I was born in South India. I am a Mathematics graduate from Madras University. I am a trained teacher and taught in India for seven years. I was brought up in a traditional Hindu way of life and underwent an arranged marriage which has survived for 33 years. I have one daughter who is a chartered accountant living in Sydney, Australia.

My Life in Britain – Career Development

1967 – 1969   Laboratory Technician

1969 – 1982   Teacher in Birmingham, progressed to Head of Department and Deputy Head.

1982 to date   Headteacher of a girls' comprehensive school, the first Asian headteacher

Vasanthi Rao

Fluent in *Hindi, Kannada, English*

Religion *Hindu*

Since 1970 I have worked in the community in various capacities. I am a member of the National Council of Women, Indian Ladies Club and Victim Support Group. I work on a voluntary basis with the Imperial Cancer Research Charity and the UK Asian Women's Centre. I am invited to give talks on various topics on education, multicultural issues, equal opportunities and travel. I have taken part in many radio and television programmes.

I help in many fundraising events, including participation in sponsored events. I support the Duke of Edinburgh Award Scheme. I went to St James' Place twice with students who were receiving Gold Awards and met Prince Philip.

Achievements & Contributions

1970	President of the Indian Ladies Club
1972 to date	Trustee, now Vice Chair, of the Birmingham Ethnic Education and Advisory Service
1974 – 1976	President/Secretary of the Asian Teachers' Association
1982	Invited by the High Commissioner of India to meet Mrs Indira Gandhi, Prime Minister of India
1983	Invited to join the Swann Committee
1983	Invited to the Inauguration of the National Rubella Campaign, in the presence of the Princess of Wales
1984	Trustee of the Prince's Trust. Met Prince Charles. Invited to a Garden Party at Buckingham Palace.
1986	Arranged a Youth Exchange Programme between British-born Indian students and Indian students from Delhi, with teachers. Three more visits took place in the subsequent years.
1987	Secretary of the Black Headteachers and Deputy Headteachers' National Association
1988	Member of the UK/USA pilot study visits which was a follow up of the visit to the USA by Kenneth Baker (then Education Secretary). As part of this programme I was invited to the White House to meet President Reagan.
1993	Appointed as a Non Executive Director of Good Hope Hospital NHS Trust. Elected Chairperson of the UK Asian Women's Conference Birmingham Branch.

Personal Interests

I enjoy living in Birmingham which has been my home for the last 27 years. I enjoy theatres, concerts, gardening and reading. I keep fit by regular walking and swimming. I have many friends from different backgrounds and I enjoy being with people.

Krishna Ray

Fluent in *Bengali, Gujarati, Hindi,*
                Punjabi, Marathi, English

My Journey

I was born in Delhi, capital city of India. I had the opportunity to live in various parts of India, since my father worked in the Indian Air Force. I graduated from the Punjab University and postgraduated from Kanpur University (UP India). I acquired a degree in vocal classical music from Allahabad University through private examinations. I came to Britain in July 1979.

My Life in Britain

My first job was as an administrative assistant at a Jewish company at Kings Cross within two months of my arrival in Britain.

In 1980 I became a library assistant in the City of Westminster Libraries. I worked there until 1983 when I had to leave to look after my newly born baby. During the period when I stayed at home, I made use of my time by teaching Indian vocal music with harmonium to girls and women of different ages. Then in December 1984 I took up a full-time job as a Co-ordinator of a Women's Group in Haringey. This group was funded by the Women's Unit of the Greater London Council.

In 1986 I joined Croydon Libraries as the Ethnic Minorities Information Officer and have worked there ever since.

I develop links with ethnic minority groups in Croydon and ensure that they are aware of the services available from libraries. I promote the library service to these groups both in the libraries and in a variety of community group meeting places through talks, promotional events, storytimes and so on, and select books for the libraries in a number of community languages. I deal with a range of enquiries relating to ethnic minority issues, for example information on the cultural background of various groups.

Achievements & Contributions

I work as a casual translator in Hindi for London Borough of Merton.

I work in films and ghazals as a public performer in Indian music. I run music workshops at schools/community centres and libraries.

I write stories in English for a bilingual magazine named *Probashi*.

Hamida Rizvi

My Journey

I was born in Agra India, but started my education in Pakistan. My father, the late Syed Damasul Hasan Rizvi, was a religious person and started my education with religion. He strongly believed in women's equality and rested his ideals in my life. He encouraged me in my educational and intellectual interests. He taught me Tajweed, the skills of reading Qur-an properly, and guided me to learn by heart. My forefathers were Iranian so my father taught me Persian literature at a very early age. It was under the influence of Persian literature and moral philosophy that I formed my own philosophy of life which is a combination of Islamic, Greek and western moral philosophies. I believe that we do not live 'by bread alone'. I strongly believe in freedom of thought and speech for everyone and respectability and equality for women, irrespective of race, colour and religion.

I graduated from Gort College for Women in Sialkot. I achieved MA in English at Murray College in Sialkot and MA in Urdu in Punjab University.

My Life in Britain

I married in 1968 and came to England after six weeks. I did not do anything for a year except writing a few poems and a long short story. I was very sad and homesick. I started working full time as a qualified graduate teacher. I stopped working when I had my first child in November 1970. I had my second son in 1972. I worked as a part-time casual artist for the External Urdu Service at the BBC from 1973 to 1974. I took a PGCE in 1975 (London). I moved to the south coast and did some part-time work in Worthing from 1976 to 1980 when I came back to Kingston in London. I did a management course in 1981 and undertook voluntary work in Kingston. I had my third son in 1983. Worked part time in Wandsworth Council's recreation service for youth and community plus voluntary teaching of Muslim women to give them awareness of the host society. I worked for Kingston Council for Racial Equality as an executive committee member for five years.

I am still working voluntarily for different groups in Kingston. I have started a weekend school for community languages. Our students passed GCSE in Urdu for the last two years. We have plans to start 'A' level classes in Urdu. I am working as a full-time lecturer for Hammersmith and Fulham Council. I am a representative of SECRE and an executive member of the Services Liaison Committee in Kingston.

I have had a hard life struggling to carry on doing social work and look after my family. I want to live as an individual, free to think and say whatever I want. I am not ready to accept that men are any better than women or that they have a right to torture a woman mentally and physically. I am a feminist. I faced heartbreak and suffering because of typical Asian culture. Still I am glad to bring up my children the way I wanted. My sons believe in respecting women and having a relationship based on mutual self-respect, love, care, understanding and support. I believe men and women should compliment each other not compete with each other. They should be like equal partners of life.

Achievements & Contributions
During my academic life in college I achieved a distinction in Persian and Islamic Studies, a prize for best essay writing, a medal and college colour for being President of Urdu Debating Society, a gold medal for best declamation, first prize for best poetry writing, a prize for being first woman editor of the College magazine in the 70-year history of the college, first prize in essay writing, a gold medal for winning two first prizes in inter-university public speaking competition, a trophy for winning English and Urdu debating competition for two years and first prize for poetry writing and best contribution for college magazine. A special golden trophy was awarded to me at Marney College Centenary Celebration in 1990 when I was declared as the best overall student of the college.

Personal Interests
I have had some books of stories and poems published. At the moment in my job I am planning a reading series and teaching material for speakers of Urdu, Hindi and Punjabi.

Shirley Rizvi

Fluent in *Urdu, Punjabi, Persian, English*

My Journey

I was educated in Lahore where I obtained BA Honours with Distinction in 1969 and MA English Literature in 1970. I started my professional career as a freelance radio broadcaster for Radio Pakistan, Lahore. In 1971 I decided to travel and went to visit my brother in Iran. It was in Iran that I decided to take up journalism and started work at the *Tehran Journal.* Because of my close ties with the Pakistani community, I found myself teaching English Literature at the Pakistan School and College.

In 1975 I married journalist Sajid Rizvi. After the birth of my son Asad in 1976 I gave up work and devoted two years to nurturing my son. During this period my husband was fully involved with covering the Iranian Revolution for United Press International and our home became a virtual press centre for visiting correspondents. It was a period of great tension in Tehran. I worked as a freelancer, first for the Italian News Agency ANSA, then for UPITN news crews in Tehran. After the fall of the Shah, I returned to full-time work in 1979 when I was Foreign Editor of the daily *Tehran Times.* The US Embassy hostage crisis soon followed, making our lives as foreign journalists in Iran extremely difficult and by July 1980 we were forced to leave Tehran.

My husband's work next took us to Turkey, which at the time was going through a terrible period with violent incidents in the streets. The Turkish military coup in September 1980 led us to leave Istanbul for Ankara where I hoped to pick up the pieces of my professional life. The coup, however, had put a heavy lid on the press in Turkey and I found myself spending most of my time studying the art and architectural riches of that country.

My Life in Britain

In 1981 another work transfer for my husband brought us to Britain. I joined the Dimbleby Newspaper Group in Richmond. I was given charge of two of the group's titles the *Brentford, Chiswick and Isleworth Times* and the *Hounslow, Feltham and Hanworth Times*.

In 1992 I joined Britain's first Asian daily newspaper the *Awaz International* as the editor of its English section. Here I found endless possibilities to present a paper for the Asian community in Britain which was devoid of bias or communal prejudice. Unfortunately in 1994 the *Awaz* folded.

In the meantime my husband and I had been developing our own publishing operations, first with *Academic File*, an international syndication service focused on the Middle East and South Asia, and then with *Eastern Art Report*, an international visual arts magazine we launched in 1989. *Academic File* was received enthusiastically by its newspaper subscribers and I was able to give full expression to my ideas on a variety of subjects including politics, the environment and the arts. The demise of *Awaz* allowed me to devote my energies full time as Executive Editor and Co-

publisher, with my husband, of *Eastern Art Report*. It allows me a platform for the multicultural ideals which have inspired me throughout my professional life.

Achievements & Contributions

At *Awaz* I had a free hand to visualise, design and decide the editorial content of the paper. I strove to present a publication which would respond to the needs of Britain's multi-faith and multicultural groups and provide a platform of understanding and goodwill for the various minority communities of this country. I sought to present *Awaz* as a campaigning newspaper on a series of issues from racism to religious intolerance. This campaigning spirit is very much the essence of the discussion and debate related to art and culture in *Eastern Art Report*.

Personal Interests

I feel committed to the issues which affect women's lives. In addition to visual arts, I have a great interest in performing arts especially music of Asian origin. One of my greatest passions is cooking. I enjoy combining different culinary ideas from various parts of the world to create something new. Most of all I feel that my lifetime experience as a professional woman and mother has given me insights that I like to share more and more with my Asian female friends.

Sarita Sabharwal

Fluent in *Hindi, Urdu, Punjabi, English*

Religion *Hindu*

My Journey

My family hails from India and I was born in New Delhi. My childhood was mostly spent in Delhi where I passed my schooling from a Government Girls' School and graduated from Delhi University in English, Hindi, Economics and Political Science.

Besides academic interests, I loved taking part in extra-curricular activities such as sports, music, dance and drama. I was an active candidate of the National Cadet Corps which trains boys and girls in sport, camping and paramilitary activities such as trekking. I was also fond of music, art and dance. I took a diploma course (sangeet visharad) from Prayaag Sangeet Samiti Allahabaad in vocal classical music. I worked as a singer and drama artist for All India Radio, Delhi youth programme for five years, during my high school and college years.

During this time I met my husband and got married to the man of my dreams. I came to London and settled here. By God's grace I was blessed with three lovely children, two boys and a girl. My husband being very supportive and co-operative helped me.

My Life in Britain

1975 – 1985   Control clerk

1985 – 1987   Accounts Department of an engineering company

1987 – 1992   Reconciliation officer for the Community Charge for Ealing Council

| 1992 – 1994 | Radio presenter/producer with Radio Asia |
| 1992 to date | Hosting the morning breakfast programme for TV Asia, including research work. I have interviewed many leading and great personalities. I have compered many shows in town and abroad. |

shows as well as helping out at charity events. I like to promote my own culture and values.

Achievements & Contributions

1992	Namaste Gold Award for services to the community awarded by the School of Cultural Heritage
1993	Community Award from the Asian Film Academy
1993	Best female presenter in the Asian DJ Awards awarded by Entasia Management
1994	Services to the Community Award from Indian Council of World Affairs. Special Award from Sukhdev Dhillon Bhangra Show. Best female presenter in the Movie Poll Awards. Also nominated for best female radio presenter.

Personal Interests

I enjoy reading, listening to music, reading poetry and writing my own, and meeting people. I also enjoy cooking, socialising and try to keep fit. I get personal enjoyment from comparing

Shahwar Sadeque

My Journey
I was born in 1942, the daughter of the late Ali Imam and of Akhtar Imam. I married Pharhad Sadeque in 1962 and have one son and one daughter. I attended Dhaka University, Bangladesh where I achieved a BSc (Hons) in Physics.

My Life in Britain
I attended Bedford College, London, achieving an MPhil in Physics and Kingston University achieving an MSc in Information Technology.

1969 – 1973	Computer Programmer with Baric Services Ltd
1973 – 1984	Teacher at Nonsuch High School, Sutton
1985 – 1992	Researcher in computer integrated manufacture incorporating vision systems and artificial intelligence at Kingston University
1990 to date	Governor of BBC

Achievements & Contributions

1989 – 1993	Member of Commission for Racial Equality
1991 to date	Member of various VAT Tribunals (England and Wales)
1991 to date	Member of Waltham Forest Housing Action Trust
1992 to date	Member of ICT (Income and Corporation Tax) Tribunals

I have had various papers published including: 'Education and Ethnic Minorities', 'Manufacturing – Towards the 21st Century' and 'A Knowledge-Based System for Sensor Interaction and Real-Time Component Control'.

Personal Interests
Collecting thimbles and perfume bottles and cooking Indian-style. I have a passion for keeping up-to-date with current affairs.

Usha Saxena

Fluent in	*Hindi, Urdu, Punjabi, English*
Religion	*Hindu*

My Journey

I was born and brought up in a multilingual and multicultural society in the state of Uttar Pradesh. My father was a practising homeopath and a Justice of the Peace. I have two brothers and four sisters.

I graduated with a BA from St Andrew's College and then attained an MA in English from University of Gorakhpur in 1962. I then joined the university as a lecturer in English until my marriage in 1967. My move to the West was necessitated on account of my marriage to a person settled in the UK. My husband is a senior civil servant.

My Life in Britain

1967 – 1968   Whilst waiting for my overseas qualifications to be recognised by the Department of Education, I passed the Civil Services examination and joined the Ministry of Social Security where I worked for about a year

1968 – 1971   Served as a peripatetic teacher at various levels in NW London and developed a keen interest in teaching young children
Also attended a course in teaching English as a second language

1971 – 1991   Primary school teacher in Borough of Merton

1991 to date	Senior Home School Liaison Teacher for early years (age three to seven) bilingual children. Currently working in Merton Early Years Language Project

Achievements & Contributions

I have presented programmes on Early Years Education on various community radio stations. I have served as a member of the executive on various community organisations including South London Hindu Society, Asian Mela Forum, Asian Arts and Culture Society and am a serving member of Wandsworth Standing Advisory Committee on Religious Education. I am also a member of the consultative committee for setting up a bakery for the elderly population in a deprived area of Guyana and raised over £7,000 through a charity concert for the initial setting up.

I organised and compered a charity concert in aid of victims of flood relief in Bangladesh in 1989 which raised more than £700. I have also organised and compered a charity concert in aid of victims of the earthquake in Maharashtra, India which raised over £3,200 and have organised various Kavi Sammelans (Hindi poetry competitions). In recognition of these services I was invited to attend first International Hindi Seminar held in Manchester under the patronship of His Excellency, Dr LM Singhvi, the High Commissioner for India.

I am serving as a Cultural Secretary of Kaprtta Sabha of London, a community organisation for the uplift of young people.

I have translated education policies and various other documents in Hindi for the London Borough of Merton.

Personal Interests

I enjoy writing short stories and Hindi poems, some of which are currently in print. I have written some multilingual books for young children based on the National Curriculum and am planning to publish a series of books with the titles *Deepak the Basket Maker, Deepak goes on a Picnic* and *Deepak Celebrates a Birthday*.

I enjoy keeping fit and swim regularly. I also enjoy cooking different types of food and have given various demonstrations on Indian cookery.

Vandana Saxena

Fluent in   *Hindi, English, French, Romanian*

Religion   *Hindu*

My Journey

I was born in St George's Hospital, Tooting and have lived in South London all my life. My education began at Beecholme Primary School where I remained until I was nine years old. I attended Streatham Hill and Clapham High School, where I was form captain and represented the school at public speaking and debating competitions. I also helped organise a number of charity functions. I left there in 1987 with ten 'O' levels. At 16, I moved to the City of London School for Girls, where I did my 'A' levels.

I spent a lot of time working at a nearby school for handicapped children. I organised an International Soiree which was attended by well over 500 people and had dances from all over the globe. This has become an annual function at the school.

After completing three 'A' levels, I read Accountancy at the London Guildhall University, where I was actively involved with representing students' views to the Board of Studies and Accountancy Department. I was also Vice-President of the Accounts Society. I graduated with an Upper Second degree and gained a BA (Hons) in Accountancy and Finance. I started on a three year training contract with chartered accountants, HW Fisher & Company. I passed my intermediate examinations in the first attempt. I sat my finals in December 1995, and gained the Chartered Accountancy qualification.

My Life in Britain

Having been born and brought up in South London, one would expect my roots to be more Western than Eastern, but this is simply not so. At an early age (about eight years old), I felt it was important for me to learn how to read and write my mother tongue, Hindi. At the same time as reading Enid Blyton I was also reading the Ramayan and Gita, as I was interested in learning about my religion and culture. Whilst enjoying listening to the sounds of Abba, I was also listening to Indian film songs. I enjoyed dancing at discos and learning Kathak. I was determined to find a medium between the two cultures and prove this could be done successfully.

I noticed, when I was 15, that a lot of my Asian friends were finding it hard to achieve the balance between being Indian and English. So I approached the Local Hindu Society and founded a youth club. It started with six people, but grew rapidly to over 40 within a matter of months. I organised and choreographed fashion shows and other functions, with over 600 people in attendance. The council noticed the work that I was doing and so I liaised with them to secure a £2,000 grant to fund activities at the youth club and arrange summer playschemes to look after Asian children. I started presenting a radio show on the local Asian radio, especially geared at teenagers. It was so successful I was asked to present similar shows on five other stations.

In the future I would like to set up my own import-export business of traditionally made textiles and clothing in a modern style, between India and the UK, in order to help those less fortunate back home in India. My ambition in life is to prove that Asian women growing up in the West are extremely able and talented in both professional careers and artistic fields. There is nothing they are not capable of.

Achievements & Contributions

I have won many prizes and been highly commended for public speaking and debating. I won an 800th Anniversary award from the Lord Mayor of the City of London to study business structure in less-developed countries.

I have written, arranged, directed and produced many plays revolving around Asian family life in the Western world. I am the arts and entertainment's editor of *The Asian* newspaper and I cover all events and exhibitions which may be of interest to Asians. I have arranged numerous charity functions. I trained in classical dance and often perform at schools giving children a flavour of the style of Kathak. I have compered and danced at various Melas over London. I am at present in the process of writing a book.

Personal Interests

I enjoy Kathak dancing, photography, swimming, writing poetry and articles, organising events for charity, talking, radio work, lateral thinking and travelling.

Saroj Bala Seth

Fluent in *Hindi, Urdu, Punjabi, Gujarati, Swahili, English*

Religion *Hindu*

My Journey

I was born in Kisumu, Kenya. My grandfather came to Kenya from Punjab (India) before the First World War. My father married my mother in 1939 in Punjab and both parents came to Kenya. I was educated in Kisumu and did my teacher training in Nairobi at Highridge Teacher Training College. My life in Kenya was very carefree with a beautiful climate all year round. I spent most of my life outdoors pursuing sports like hockey, tennis, netball and badminton. I taught in a large co-education primary school where I participated fully in all aspects of school life both social and educational. After the independence of Kenya I was the only teacher in my school who was given responsibility to teach Swahili. Multilingualism was the norm and multiculturalism and the multi-faith aspect became the everyday way of life for the society.

My Life in Britain

I came to Britain in July 1967 and began my teaching career in September of the same year. Having taught in a Church of England primary school for nearly three and a half years, I moved to Leicester with my family. Since April 1971 I have taken an active part serving both the statutory and voluntary sector bringing in a lot of changes for the better. I put equal opportunities issues on the agenda of Leicestershire politics in the early 1970s. I have been actively involved in politics and have contested a City Council seat in Leicester. I was invited to a garden party in July 1988 at Buckingham Palace.

Career Development

1967 – 1970	Class teacher at St Clements CE Primary School in London N7
1971 – 1972	Class teacher at Duxbury Primary School in Leicester
1973 – 1982	Head of department for ESL support at Uplands Infant School
1971 – 1982	Taught English as a Second Language to Asian adults
1978 – 1982	Taught Hindustani to adults who worked directly with the Asian communities
1982 – 1992	Advisory teacher for bilingual education and head of the bilingual team based at the Centre for Multicultural Education
1992 to date	Section Eleven project leader with responsibility for 45 staff and 20 schools

Achievements & Contributions

I have been a Justice of the Peace since 1982 and worked on the Juvenile Bench from 1985 to 1991.

I am an advisor to the Afro Caribbean and Asian Forum Race Relations Committee and a member of the Probation Offender Forum.

In 1989 I represented the Leicester City Bench on the Child Protection Committee and in 1991 I worked on the Shadow Family Panel Bench.

Since 1993 I have been a non-executive member of the Management Committee of 'Sabras' Asian Radio.

Since 1994 I have been a member of the Advisory Panel for Ethnic Minorities at Leicester General Hospital for patient care.

I have attended a variety of courses and conferences during my career. I am currently working on recommendations pertaining to Black and Asian women for Leicestershire County Council's various committees.

Personal Interests

I enjoy living in Leicester because of its very positive multicultural environment. I love cooking and experimenting with dishes from other parts of the world. I lead a very active social life but most of my time is occupied working in the evenings for various committees in the private, voluntary and statutory sectors. I enjoy reading and like to keep up with the current issues. I have a very wide circle of friends of all nationalities with whom I meet regularly.

My Journey

I was born in Sydney, Australia. My family is originally from Peshawar in the North-West Frontier of Pakistan. During the late 1950s, my father joined the Ministry of Foreign Affairs, Pakistan. His first posting was in Sydney where my parents lived for five years. I was a late and much-wanted first baby to which I owe a memorable and beautiful 'designer' childhood. My first language was English.

During the mid 1960s we spent our second posting in Khartoum, Sudan, where I became fluent in Arabic. We travelled Europe and during the 1970s we settled in London, for the purpose of good schooling. I have a passion for the Urdu language and have maintained this rigorously.

Aziza Alaud-Din Shah

Fluent in *Urdu, Hindi, English, and a good understanding of Arabic*

Religion *Muslim*

My Life in Britain

1982 – 1984   Personal Assistant to the Ambassador of Yemen in London

1984 – 1985   Assistant Secretary to the Zakat Committee at the Islamic Cultural Centre, London

1986 – 1990   Lecturer-in-Charge of the Information Technology Section at Richmond Adult College

1990 – 1992   Acting Deputy Head of Department, Business Studies and Languages Richmond Adult College

Achievements & Contributions

1986 Postgraduate Certificate in Further Education, London

1993 Masters Degree in Educational Studies, London. Dissertation research on 'Giving the Will to Learn – A Study in Holistic Education'. Extracts to be published in British Educational Journals.

Conducted seminars at the British Film Institute for management staff on 'Women and HIV Awareness'

Participant at seminars organised at the House of Lords on International Peace and Conflict Resolution

1994 Consultant on Women and Islam to the Ghandi Foundation, School of Non-Violence .

Assisting with a feasibility study into the establishment of the Commonwealth Council for Conflict Resolution (University of London)

Acting Advisor on Islamic ethics to the International Institute for Peace and Global Ethics

Public Relations Assistant to Ismail Merchant, Film Director, London

Interviewed by BBC World Service on 'Sufistic' tradition of Qawwali music from Pakistan

1995 Acting Personal Assistant to Thomas C Daffern, Secretary-General of the World Conference on Religion and Peace and Director of the International Institute for Peace and Global Ethics

Personal Interests

I live in a large old Victorian house in Clapham Common with my parents. Home decorating and shopping are long-standing passions, and we have been slowly renovating the house for the last ten years. I spend a great deal of time in Central London however, and hope to make this my ultimate home base.

My social circle comprises mainly Middle Eastern friends who have been catalysts in enriching and enlightening my life. I socialise intensely and in particular adore foreign movies, theatre, dinners/balls and spontaneous events. Keeping fit is an important part of my routine and I love circuit training and cycling during the summer. I collect minerals and belong to the Amateur Mineral Collectors Society. I take a keen interest in cultural activities and maintain links with the Pakistan Embassy. Travelling abroad is always a tempting lure away from London and I indulge myself as often as inspiration and circumstances allow to scan new horizons and cultures.

Najma Shah

| **Fluent in** | *Hindi, Urdu, Punjabi, English* |

| **Religion** | *Muslim* |

My Journey

I was born in India. My family migrated to Lahore, Pakistan after Partition in 1947. My early education was in Pakistan. Bilingualism was considered natural and everyone was able to speak a local dialect as well as Urdu, which was the official language. As a child I was speaking Punjabi at home, Urdu at school and was reading Arabic as part of the religious education. At the age of ten, English and Farsi were included in my school curriculum. I sustained my interest in English and in 1965 I completed an MA degree in English Language and Literature.

My Life in Britain

1965 – 1969	Teacher of English at Victoria High School
1970 – 1972	Adult education and nursery adviser, Nigeria
1972 – 1975	Tutor of English as a second language AEI
1975 – 1976	Retrained for primary teaching PGCE London
1976 – 1986	Teaching and management posts in three schools
1986 – 1989	Adviser on Multicultural Education for ILEA
1989 to date	Primary phase inspector, Haringey LEA

Achievement & Contributions

I have been actively involved in voluntary work throughout my life. I helped to establish many self-help community organisations in London. Through the work of these organisations I have created a network of mutual support and opportunities for training and education for women. Work with voluntary groups involves close collaboration with a variety of institutions and personnel. My main contribution to charity work is the establishment of a Women's Resource Centre in Southwark, where women are able to learn new skills to improve the quality of their lives.

I am also very committed to improving the provision and quality of nursery education for under fives.

I was the Chairperson of the ILEA Consultative Committee for Black and Ethnic Minority communities.

I am involved in raising funds for a wide range of charities.

Personal Interests

I enjoy living in London. The cosmopolitan nature of the city has offered me the opportunities to make friends from diverse social, cultural and racial backgrounds. I like cooking for friends and sharing views with people.

Dr Annapoorna Sharma MSC, MBBS MRCP, DCH

Fluent in *Hindi, Sanskrit, English*

Religion *Hindu*

My Journey

I was born in London, while my parents were pursuing postgraduate studies at university. By the age of five I was a fluent reader of English and Sanskrit and was filmed by the BBC. We returned to India and my father became a Member of Parliament (Lok Sabha) defeating the then Home Minister by fifty *lakh* (5,000,000) votes. I was educated at the Convent of Jesus and Mary, New Delhi, and at home met many political figures. My home environment has always been politically aware and active.

At 16 I returned to London where I attended Godolphin and Latymer School and went on to Middlesex Hospital Medical School (now part of UCL) where I qualified in 1980. I have spent some time at the All India Institute of Medical Sciences, Delhi, and at the John Hopkins University, Baltimore, USA. Most of my postgraduate career has been in London teaching hospitals and I am now a consultant paediatrician in London.

My Life in Britain

1975 – 1980   Medical student at University College Hospital Medical School

1980 – 1981   House Officer to Sir Douglas Ranger and Sir William Slack, Deans of Middlesex Hospital Medical School

1983 – 1984   Neonatal Paediatrics, University College Hospital, London

1984 – 1985	Rotating Registrar, Paediatrics at Queen Elizabeth Hospital for Sick Children, Great Ormond Street Hospital for Sick Children Group
1988 – 1992	Senior Registrar, Paediatrics at Royal Free Hospital, London
1991 – 1992	Medical Research Council studentship award for Epidemiology at London School of Hygiene and Tropical Medicine
1992 – 1996	Senior Clinical Medical Officer and Head of School Health Service, Camden and Islington Community NHS Trust
1996 to date	Consultant Paediatrician, Queen Charlotte's and Chelsea Hospital and Royal Postgraduate Medical School

Achievements & Contributions

Numerous lectures and seminars to medical students, postgraduates, GPs and nursing staff on all aspects of paediatrics. I am a keen and enthusiastic teacher.

In 1995 I chaired the conference on 'The New British Child' at the Royal Postgraduate Medical School. I co-wrote *Meeting the Needs of Refugee Children: a checklist for children in Camden Schools,* 1996

I am a member of the School Health Working Party Camden, the Camden Under Fives committee and the Primary child health services management committee.

Personal Interests

I am married and I have a small son and a daughter. I enjoy English literature, walking in the country, Indian and western classical music and teaching medical students. I like gardening, especially in the style of Vita Sackville-West and Gertrude Jekyll. Paediatrics is my hobby. I enjoyed very much living and working and being a medical student in Camden; I was a school doctor and eventually the supervisor of the school doctor at the same primary school where I first learned to write in Camden. I return to India as often as I can and I retain a keen interest in politics.

My Journey

I was born in Pakistan in 1966. I came to Britain at the age of four and have remained here since. Being very much influenced by my late father who was an accomplished barrister, I learned early the importance and power of education, and struggled to achieve the same level of success as my father. As I grew up I remember that, although I was the youngest member of the family, with two older brothers and two older sisters, we were always considered equals by our parents, regardless of age or gender. The significance of that equality is very apparent to me now.

Having been influenced by two very diverse cultures, I consider myself to be British and Asian in equal measures, and by drawing positive elements from both cultures, combine them to create a happy medium which allows me to have the 'best of both worlds'.

Asmat Sheikh

Fluent in *Urdu, Punjabi, English*

Religion *Muslim*

My Life in Britain

1982 Ten GCE 'O' levels

1990 BTEC Ordinary National Diploma in Fashion Design

1994 BA (Hons) in Fashion: Design and Marketing at the University of East London

On completion of my degree, a number of avenues were open to me. My ultimate goal is to become an international label, and to be considered as a successful British Asian designer of subcultural fashion (East meets West) on equal terms with the recognised British designers of the British fashion industry.

Achievements & Contributions

My father would say, 'Reach for the moon and you may catch a few stars...' I think I have managed to catch a few of the stars ...but I continue to reach for the moon!

April 1990	Nelbarden Cup for Swimwear Design
January 1993	Special Commendation in Libas Fashion Design Competition
Nov 1993	Network East/Cineblitz Asian Designer of the Year Award

At present I am working in conjunction with the Commission for Racial Equality who have shown considerable interest in my final year thesis. This is based on the absence of Asian designer names within the British fashion industry and the Commission are providing me with funding for more research to be carried out. This is a highly important issue to me personally as it directly affects my future aspirations of becoming a recognised British Asian designer. Since winning the Network East/Cineblitz Designer of the Year Award I have contributed to radio programmes on Greater London Radio and television fashion programmes on TV Asia. I have consequently been given a regular fashion programme on TV Asia on Sky Television.

Personal Interests

I have an avid interest in all the international designers with regards to their advertising, management, lifestyle and collections. I have been a former member of the school netball, badminton, fencing and chess teams. I have a keen interest in crafts such as tambour beading, embroidery, appliqué and handpainted fabrics. I really enjoy producing pastille portraits and painting for relaxation. I am also a compulsive chocaholic and shopaholic!

Ayesha Sheikh

Fluent in *French, German, Urdu, English*

Religion *Muslim*

My Journey

I was born in London in 1974. My great-grandparents migrated to Lahore, Pakistan from Kashmir. My father, after graduating from Government College, Lahore in 1967, came to London for higher studies. He then entered into international trading and established his own company here. In 1992, he married my mother, Nusrat Yasmin, who was a lecturer in English at Islamia College.

Achievements & Contributions

I was always active in all parts of school life. I was elected Form Leader every year. I also played in the hockey and netball teams, the gymnastics squad, sang in the choir, raised money for Form charities, debated and participated in plays, both on and off stage. At 14, I wrote a play that was translated into Latin and performed in an inter-schools competition, where it won second prize. At 16, I won a School Prize for my achievements in GCSEs.

I was elected Head Girl at Wimbledon High School by staff and students. My duties were varied and often quite demanding, but also a lot of fun. My position involved organising many events, a great deal of public speaking, and even more tact for liaising between staff and students. Some of the events I organised included a ball for Sixth Formers, a charity lunch for teachers, a leavers' assembly and a revue involving staff and pupils at the end of the year. I was also editor of creative writing for the school magazine.

I worked with a class of 12 year olds when

I led a drama group. Our work culminated in the production of a play which I jointly directed and produced. I participated in community service by helping to organise parties for blind children, helping at Christian Care outings and by visiting an elderly house-bound lady regularly to do her shopping. In July 1990 I made a parachute jump from 2,500 feet. I won prizes for gaining A grades in my 'A' Levels and for being Head Girl.

I am still in education. I am doing a BA Honours degree in English Language and Literature at Somerville College, Oxford.

In 1994 I was President of the Oxford University Majlis, a historic society that was founded in 1896 to agitate for the independence of the Indian subcontinent. It continues to promote Asian culture, society and interests as well as cater for the needs of the South Asian students. During my presidency, I organised a charity dinner in aid of the South Asian Development Partnership, which was attended by several dignitaries including the High Commissioner of Pakistan, a careers evening, a mehfil-e-mushaira, debates, seminars and social gatherings. I represent my college at the Joint Consultative Committee (JCC) of the English Faculty Board. As a member of a home-teaching scheme of the Joint Action Against Racial Intolerance (JACARI), I have been regularly teaching Bengali girls who have been under-performing at school. I have won prizes for speaking at the Somerville Debating Society. In February 1992 I represented Pakistan in a model United Nations held by the Oxford University Union Society in which the resolution reached by our delegation on the 'Kashmir Issue' gained widespread coverage by the media.

Personal Interests

As a linguist with a palate for foreign food and a keen interest in different cultures, I love travelling and have been lucky enough to have travelled around the world. Countries which I have found the most fascinating are Japan, China and Hawaii.

As a student of literature, I am naturally a voracious reader, and can definitely testify to the immortal words of Longfellow that "Art is long and time is fleeting".

Photography is another interest that I wish I had more time for. I have taken courses in this and can develop and print my own film. I was briefly involved in taking photographs for the *Oxford Student*. I also enjoy going to the cinema and theatre, especially to see foreign or art productions.

Sofia Sheikh

Fluent in *Hindi, Urdu, Punjabi, English*

Religion *Muslim*

My Journey

I was born in Malaysia of Asian origin parentage. My paternal grandfather migrated from India and settled in Malaysia around in the 1890s.

I spent 20 years in Malaysia and was educated at a convent school. My childhood days were the best years of my life. I remember having a freedom of life with no social pressures.

I came to the UK in 1969 to further my career.

My Life in Britain

1969 – 1973	Undertook three years State Registered Nurse training
1973 – 1974	Midwifery training (one year course)
1975 – 1979	Worked as a Midwifery Sister in Croydon
1979 – 1980	Undertook Health Visitor's training at Ewell College, Surrey
1980 to date	Practice as a Health Visitor in Croydon, Wimbledon, Haringey and Barnet

Achievements & Contributions

In 1991 I produced an Asian weaning and diet package for Barnet.

In 1992 I was involved in a research project looking into coronary heart disease within the Asian community in the area where I practice.

I work very closely with the Asian population looking into their health needs and am involved in health promotion and education. For this I am closely connected with the Sangam Asian Advice Centre.

At present I am working as a TB Co-ordinator gaining experience in tuberculosis work.

I have worked as a District Nurse in the community in Barnet where I am also the community ethnic resource person.

I have gained experience working in nursing homes with the elderly, homeless families and battered women's refuge.

I work very closely with Sangam Asian Advice Centre in Edgware and other voluntary organisations.

I am involved in health education in schools, contributing to Asian radio programmes.

Personal Interests

I enjoy living in North London which has a large multicultural ethnic population. I enjoy cooking different types of food especially Far Eastern dishes. I have a wide circle of friends from different ethnic backgrounds and we often discuss health, educational and political issues.

Yasmin Sheikh

Fluent in *Gujarati, Hindi, Urdu, Punjabi, Swahili, English*

Religion *Muslim*

My Journey

I was born in East Africa. My ancestors migrated to Lahore, Pakistan from Kashmir. My father left Lahore in 1920 at the age of 20, to visit his elder brother who had a tea plantation in Tanzania.

I spent 23 years in Tanzania and was educated at Government Secondary School. I remember life was full of freedom, in speech and movement – no pressures, no political tensions, lovely beaches, watersports and swimming with friends. Being part of a multilingual and multicultural society was enriching. Just before I left political awareness developed and we mixed with friends speaking the native tongue called Swahili.

My Life in Britain

1965 – 1971	Primary school teacher in Leicester and London
1971 – 1988	Advisory teacher for English as a Second Language in Croydon
1988 to date	Adviser for Multicultural Education in Merton

Achievements & Contributions

1969 Invited to join the committee looking into the linguistic needs of immigrant children in schools in England and Wales

1978 Invited by Shirley Williams, then Labour Member of Parliament, to serve on the Rampton Committee became the Swann Committee of Education

1979 Invited to a Garden Tea Party at Buckingham Palace

1980 Invited by the BBC to contribute multicultural stories for children on their *You & Me* programme

1984 Involved in raising charity funds for children in developing countries

1986 Served on various educational committees, contributing towards multicultural and equal opportunities issues

1989 Contributed to Asian radio programmes

1992 Elected to the Forum which advises Croydon Council on all ethnic minority issues and matters

1993 Interviewed on television regarding the National Curriculum and multicultural education and then as part of a panel of successful women in a man's world

1993 Elected to the Education Committee in Croydon

1994 Interviewed on BBC 1 series on the Muslim community (second generation) in the UK

Invited by the BBC to contribute to a programme *The Way of Life*

1996 Awarded the Certificate of Merit for distinguished services. The personal profile will be published in the 1997 Dictionary of International Biographies.

Since 1991 I have been working on the compilation of *Not So Silent! Profiles of Successful Asian Women*.

Personal Interests
I enjoy living in Norbury, mixing with the local community and visiting local shops. Norbury has easy access to all facilities. I try to keep fit; I swim regularly and enjoy walking in the country. I like cooking different types of foods. I have a wide circle of friends from many different ethnic groups.

Rizwana Shelley

Fluent in *Urdu, English with a working knowledge of Punjabi and Farsi*

Religion *Muslim*

My Journey

I spent my childhood in Khyber and Khurram Agencies in the North West Frontier Province of Pakistan. I went to convent schools in Peshawar, Quetta and Sahiwal, Pakistan.

My Life in Britain

1961 – 1963   Passed nine 'O' levels at the Hove County Grammar School for Girls, East Sussex

1963 – 1965   Passed three 'A' levels in Physics, Pure Mathematics and Applied Mathematics at the Tiffin Girls Grammar School, Kingston upon Thames, Surrey

1965 – 1968   Gained a BSc (Hons) in Physics from Royal Holloway College (University of London)

1968 – 1971   Achieved an MSc and DIC in Physics from Imperial College of Science and Technology, University of London

1971 – 1973   Ran the electron probe microanalysis facility at the Cambridge University of Metallurgy

1985 to date   Teaching secondary pupils Physics, Chemistry, Biology and Mathematics in Chatham,

Kent. Acting Head of Science in my school. At present I am second in charge of the Science Faculty.

Achievements & Contributions

1969 – 1971	Contributed regularly to the Urdu Service of the BBC World Service
1973 – 1975	Worked on a freelance basis for the British Council in Tehran, Iran
1976 – 1978	In great demand as a speaker on Eastern culture at Butte, Montana in the USA
1978 to date	Actively involved in voluntary work for the community in the Medway Towns including mother tongue teaching. Also took part in the 'Parosi' (Neighbour) scheme.
1987/1988	Member of the Steering Committee of the North Kent Festival of Cultures
1979 – 1990	Member of the Advisory Council for BBC Radio Kent
1979 – 1987	Contributed regularly to BBC Radio Kent's *Sangam* programme for ethnic minorities
1989 – 1990	Vice Chairman of the Medway and Gillingham Community Relations Council
1990	Appointed Justice of the Peace, County of Kent

Personal Interests

I enjoy being actively involved in the community in the Medway Towns. I love entertaining, being entertained and travelling far and wide. I try to keep active by going for walks. Being a scientist I am very interested in the latest discoveries and innovations.

Saida Sherif

Fluent in *Urdu, French, English*

My Journey

I was born in Delhi. I attended Jamia Millya Islamia School. It was an all boys school and was unique in its approach to teaching. We were encouraged to debate and give speeches. At the age of eight, I used to participate in an Indian radio programme every Sunday. I also wrote my own stories and acted in plays along with Chinu Mian, Munay Mian and Mithoo Mian. The Second World War was on and I can recall hearing occasional sirens. My school and college days were fun but we had a strong instinct to compete and perform better. Then the horrible and unfair Partition of India took place. We were driven out of our homes and we fled. I went to live in Switzerland in 1948. I came to study in England in 1951 and I took part in some programmes at the BBC.

My Life in Britain

Having travelled extensively since an early age, I feel quite at home in most countries. Somehow I feel that England is where I belong. My mother was a great lady; all my inspirations and finer thoughts come through her influence. I have been on the Board of Governors for Anson School and Islamia School in London Borough of Brent. I have taught Sunday School for nearly 22 years. I have had poems, short stories and some papers on education, including one on dyslexia, published. I have endeavoured to write in all three languages. My children have far excelled me, not only in their literary work, but in all fields, leaving me a very proud and happy mother.

1949 – 1950	Interpreter in UN conference in Palais de Nations, Geneva
1956 – 1958	Worked for Air France and helped in translating IATA rules
1962 – 1964	French teacher in American School, Karachi
1964 – 1965	Headmistress in Karachi
1965 – 1967	Worked in London in a shipping company. I continued writing and broadcasting Urdu programmes from BBC World Service as a parallel activity.
1967 – 1979	Clerk at the Bank of England

Friends joined together and a literary circle called Burg-e-Gul was formed. Young and old writers were invited to read their work and a booklet was published.

1974 – 1975	Taught French at Holborn Polytechnic twice a week
1980	Taught in Manarat Jeddah International after taking early retirement from the Bank of England
1983 – 1988	Taught in North Kensington & Hammersmith Comm-

unity School and at Ayelstone Community School

1988	Interpreter and translator in English, Urdu, French and Arabic in the Department of Law & Administration, Harrow. Taught ESL in Greenhill College.

In 1993 I resigned from both jobs in order to work as a volunteer for the Convoy of Mercy. This small organisation has taken over 2,000 tons of aid and implemented various teaching programmes and rehabilitation centres in Croatia and now inside Bosnia.

Personal Interests
I loved skiing and later indulged in flower arrangements. I am a member of 13 societies who are committed to various charities and welfare work. Occasionally I have given lectures. I like to read and travel but I don't see myself travelling for fun when calamities such as Bosnia and Chechinia keep taking place in today's so-called 'civilised Europe'. I would like to quote a verse of Hafiz:

> "et je me suis écrié
> O' fortune
> le soleil est levé
> et tu dors encore
> et la fortune
> m'a repondu:
> malgré tout
> ne desespère pas".

Lian-Choo Smee

Fluent in	Chinese, English, Malay

Religion	Buddhist

My Journey

I was born in Malaysia into a traditional big Chinese family of 12. I remember life was full of freedom and fun.

My father was the landlord, but there was an open door policy for all the neighbourhood. Everyone visited each other and helped in each other's family occasions without being asked.

Malaysia is a multicultural country and there are various types of school to cater for each race's needs. All of us were educated in Chinese school with the benefits of learning English and Malay as well as mother tongue. All the schools participated in all sports and cultural events.

My Life in Britain

From 1975 to 1978 I was training to be a psychiatric nurse . The first three months in England were lonely, depressed and miserable. I was struggling very hard to cope with the demands of professional studying and settling down in the cold, unfriendly environment. It was a total culture shock for me.

Once I had settled down I was able to build up my confidence. My self-esteem strengthened after I passed my examination and was offered the post of Acting-up Ward Sister.

I've been a Senior Charge Nurse in charge at the Bethlem Royal Hospital, Beckenham at night since 1988, and duty nurse in charge of the Maudsley Hospital, Denmark Hill at night since 1992. The responsibilities are dealing with all the emergencies and ensuring high standards in the quality of nursing.

1987 onwards	Chinese advisor to multicultural education in Croydon and West Wickham
1992	Contacted and advised the Chinese community in Merton to form the Chinese Committee in Vestry Hall

Achievements & Contributions

1975	Published a book of stories and poems with friends in Malaysia
1975 – 1989	Letters from London published in Malaysia's national newspaper
1987 – 1992	Translated English children's story books into Chinese
1992 to date	Bilingual Assistant in Early Years unit in Merton on my days off from nursing

Personal Interests

I enjoy cooking and tasting different types of food, and gardening. I also try to fit in cycling and swimming when I have free time. I always take great interest in my children's educational development.

Satwant Kaur Suri

Fluent in *Hindi, Urdu, Punjabi, English*

Religion *Sikh*

My Journey

I was born in Lahore. My father settled in Lahore after leaving his village, Gunghrilla near Rawalpindi (West Punjab) now Pakistan. After Partition in 1947 when the British left India, we migrated to Simla in North India. After living there for eight years we had to leave Simla as my father had a job move to Chandigarh. Here I did my matriculation from Government Basic High School. I then completed my further studies, a BA degree and an MA degree both in Maths, from Punjab University, Chandigarh. I got married in 1963 and started teaching in Higher Secondary School, Chandigarh. My husband came to the UK in 1964 with an Employment Voucher and we finally emigrated to the UK in 1965.

My Life in Britain

1966 – 1974	Infant teacher with Inner London Education Authority
1974 – 1981	ESL Co-ordinator in a primary school in Croydon.
1982 to date	Left ESL to join mainstream education as a primary school teacher in Croydon
1986 to date	Language Co-ordinator throughout the school
1989 to date	Upper School Co-ordinator

Achievements & Contributions

1978	Received RSA Certificate for teaching English as a Second Language
1979	Elected as an executive member of our local gurdwara
1986 – 1988	Involved in a National Writing Project
1986 to date	Teacher Governor for my school
1987	Received a DES Certificate for attending a reading and language consultants' course
1993 – 1994	Involved in working parties for reading and writing assessment sheets

Personal Interests

In addition to school, I enjoy participating fully in extra-curricular activities. Since 1986 I have been raising funds for the People's Dispensary for Sick Animals with the help of the schoolchildren. In 1988 I was involved in organising an Asian Evening in school for the parents. This included a cultural programme, fashion show and food.

In 1992 a multicultural evening which I was involved in was also very successful. For the last ten years I have held a stall at our Christmas and Summer School fairs. Also for many years now I have had full responsibility for taking the children on school journeys away from home for a week.

I enjoy living in Croydon and mixing with the local community. I take an active part in our local gurdwara and organise fund-raising events for our local community. In 1980 – 1981 I arranged several sponsored walks in aid of a building fund for my local gurdwara. I have also served the local community in other ways. In 1982 I received permission from the local authority to teach Punjabi to the local children at my school in the evenings. I have also this year raised money for Relate to help children in crisis.

I like to keep fit by exercising every day and going for long walks. I enjoy cooking and sewing in my spare time. I love reading and watching TV adventure and detective stories, and also Indian plays. I have a wide circle of friends from many different ethnic groups. I also have three grown-up daughters.

Najma Usman

Fluent in *Urdu, English*

Religion *Muslim*

My Journey

I was born in Aligarh, India. After Partition my parents migrated to Karachi, Pakistan. My father was a magistrate and then moved on to practising as a lawyer.

I spent nearly 20 years in Karachi. I was educated at a Grammar School followed by a BSc and a Master's Degree in Organic Chemistry.

From early school days I took a keen interest in Urdu literature. I was a good debater and won a few prizes for my school and college.

After getting married I left Pakistan in 1969. My lifelong dream was to get a PhD in Britain (dreams never come true!).

My Life in Britain

1969 – 1973   Research Chemist at Polyalloys of Kingston, Surrey

1977 – 1980   Research Officer at Paint Research Association in Teddington Middlesex

1980 – 1990   Senior Research Officer

1990   Big switch from industry to teaching of Adult Education. Currently teaching GCSE and 'A' level Urdu, English for Science and English as a Second Language at Merton Sixth Form College and South Thames College.

Achievements & Contributions

Since 1980 I have been involved in several women's organisations and voluntary work.

1985   Interviewed by BBC External Services on Chemistry and Poetry

1986   Presented paper on 'Non Lead Driers' at the OCCA conference in Eastbourne

1987   Presented paper on 'Enzymatic Degradation of Cellulose Ethers' at the Paint Research Symposium

1989   Collection of Urdu poems published (Title *Shakhe-Hinah*)

1989   Elected Vice President of Kingston Muslim Women's Welfare Organisation

Since 1990 I have helped to organise and run Urdu language classes for muslim children in New Malden.

In 1992 I was awarded certificate in TESLA (teaching English to speakers of other languages) at Westminster College.

Personal Interests

I enjoy writing Urdu poetry and attending literary programmes. I get tremendous satisfaction from teaching Urdu to Asian children and English as a second language to refugees and bilingual students. I love cooking exotic Indian dishes. I am a keen gardener and simply adore going to Chelsea Flower Show. I have a wide selection of Urdu poetry and enjoy reading at bedtime. I have many friends from different ethnic groups. Whenever we can, we organise gatherings and talk about a wide range of subjects from cooking recipes to cultural issues, literature and the education of children.

Maria Vaz

| **Fluent in** | *English, Swahili* |

| **Religion** | *Catholic* |

My Journey

I was born in a small town called Kisumu by the shores of Lake Victoria in Kenya. My parents are from Goa and migrated to Kenya in search of better opportunities. My father set up a very successful law practice. I grew up in idyllic conditions – vast open spaces, endearing people and safety. I was sent to England to receive what my parents regarded was the best education in the world.

My Life in Britain

Having completed a degree in Law at Cardiff University College, I qualified as a barrister. Having practiced for around three years, I then briefly worked as a Justice's clerk. I then joined the UK Immigrants Advisory Service for a year and a half and then came to the City to a Solicitors' firm to found and develop an immigration law practice.

Achievements & Contributions

1991 Appointed to the Law Society's Sub Committee on Immigration

1992 Secretary to the International Bar Association's Migration and Nationality Law Committee

1994 Appointed to the Equal Opportunities Committee of the Law Society

I have written numerous articles in various legal and business journals on immigration. I write a regular column for the *Asian Times* and recently appeared on BBC Radio Scotland to discuss the new immigration rules.

Personal Interests

I enjoy watching people. I love meeting people and exchanging ideas. I like music, dancing, reading, current affairs and walking.

My Journey

Born in Tehran, Iran, I came to England for further education at the age of 18. Four years later my career in education began. I married an Englishman and returned to Iran where we lived and taught for 14 years till 1980. My two children were born in Tehran. A year after the Iranian Revolution we were compelled to come back to London. I commenced working in the language field and pursued further studies.

My Life in Britain

1965 – 1966   Biology teacher, Hackney comprehensive school

1981 – 1985   Language and Tutorial College Principal

Shahla Taheri White

1985 – 1988   Advisory teacher at the Centre for Urban Educational Studies, ILEA

Fluent in *Farsi, English*

Religion *Muslim*

1988 – 1992   Advisory Teacher at Multicultural Education and Curriculum Support Service (MECSS) in Hertfordshire (Bilingualism and Community Languages)

1992 to date   Adviser at MECSS

Achievements & Contributions

1973   Co-founded a Dual Language Co-educational International School in Tehran (650 pupils) which operated until nationalisation in 1980

1981	Set up a Language School/Tutorial College in London (open till 1985)
1981	Founded a Farsi (mother-tongue) Language School for the Iranian community in London, open on Saturdays and still thriving.
1985 – 1987	External Examiner/ Assessor for RSA
1988 to date	Chief Verifier for RSA Diploma Courses (Teaching of Community Languages)
	Occasional broadcaster, BBC World Service (Persian programme) and Spectrum radio
	Contributor to *Multilingualism in the British Isles,* published in 1991, and to various language teaching magazines and INSET training videos.
	Conference speaker/ lecturer on bilingualism and language teaching issues. Voluntary work for Iranian charities for earthquake relief and medical care

1991 – 1993	Campaigned (in vain) for the retention of Farsi as a GCE/GCSE examination subject via Friends of Persian Language Society

Personal Interests
Cooking and entertaining, travel, classical Persian dance and modern dance.

Submission Form

If you would like to see your profile in the next edition of *Not So Silent,* photocopy and complete this form. Feel free to continue on a separate sheet.

Please enclose a good quality photograph of yourself and return to: Not So Silent, Mrs Yasmin Sheikh, 15 Ederline Avenue, Norbury sw16 4rz.

Name

Address

Fluent in

Date of Birth

Religion

My Journey

Achievements & Contributions

My Life in Britain

Personal Interests